SEARCHING FOR GOD, THE PRECIOUS TREASURE IN MY DAILY LIFE

REVEREND PETER G. VU

Copyright © 2022 Reverend Peter G. Vu

All rights reserved. No part of this book may be reproduced, stored, or transmitted by any means—whether auditory, graphic, mechanical, or electronic—without written permission of both publisher and author, except in the case of brief excerpts used in critical articles and reviews. Unauthorized reproduction of any part of this work is illegal and is punishable by law.

Unless otherwise noted, scripture quotations are
taken from the following source:

The New American Bible, © 1970 by the Confraternity Christian Doctrine, Washington, D.C., including the Revised Psalms of the New American Bible, © 1991, and the Revised New Testament, © 1986. Used by permission of the copyright owner. All rights reserved.

Poems and prayers are taken from the internet, and the English translation of the "Liturgy of the Hours" is © 1970, 1973, 1975, and 1976 by the International Committee on English in the Liturgy. All rights reserved.

Pictures and illustrations are taken from www.istockphoto.com and are used by permission of the copyright owner. All rights reserved.

ISBN: 978-1-957203-56-0 (sc)
ISBN: 978-1-957203-57-7 (hc)
ISBN: 978-1-957203-58-4 (e)

Because of the dynamic nature of the Internet, any web addresses or links contained in this book may have changed since publication and may no longer be valid. The views expressed in this work are solely those of the author and do not necessarily reflect the views of the publisher, and the publisher hereby disclaims any responsibility for them.

THE EWINGS PUBLISHING

The Ewings Publishing LLC
One Galleria Blvd., Suite 1900, Metairie, LA 70001
1-888-421-2397

I would like to dedicate this book to the following groups:

- My loving and faithful God, who has always been the wonderful treasure to bring me wisdom, guidance, protection, comfort, and joy in my life.

- People who are suffering under life's burden or other personal setbacks. Your resilience and complete trust in God teaches us to come to God often and keep moving forward with a smile.

- People who are feeling lost or discouraged in modern-day culture. Your commitment and hope in divine power tells us to search for the guiding light of God in our dark nights of the soul.

- People of faith and anyone who sincerely searches for God every day. Your desire to be close to God and find purpose for your lives encourages me to write this book and find more ways for us to encounter God in our secular and materialistic society.

- I'm forever grateful to our omnipresent God and indebted to you all. May our loving and faithful God reveal God's presence throughout your day and continue to bless you and your loved ones.

CONTENTS

Introduction vii

1. Why We Need God Every Moment of Our Life; Seven Signs to Show that We Truly Have Met God: Love, Mercy, Peace, Joy, Hope, Generosity, and Faithfulness 1

2. How God Was Found in the Old Testament 32

3. How God Was Found in the New Testament 56

4. Whether God Is Still Needed in a High-Tech and Comfortable Society, and How God Can Be Found in Modern Times 76

5. How an Ordinary Person Finds God throughout the Week 83
   Monday: Finding God in a Family or a Home 85
   Tuesday: Finding God at a School, a Library, or a Center of Education 86
   Wednesday: Finding God at Work, a Repair Shop, a Bank, or a Place of Business 88
   Thursday: Finding God in a Neighborhood or a Place of Charity 90
   Friday: Finding God at a Ball Game, a Theater, or a Center of Entertainment 92

Saturday: Finding God at a Shopping Mall,
a Grocery Store, or a Public Place 94
Sunday: Finding God at a Church, a Temple,
or a Mosque 95

6. How an Ordinary Person Finds God in
   Extraordinary Situations 98
   Tragedies 98
   Sickness 100
   Broken relationships 101
   Daily Problems 102
   Other Unusual Situations 103

INTRODUCTION

There are many topics I want to write and many issues I wish to discuss with the people of God. But after some talks with friends and prayerful consideration, I have decided to write this book: *Searching for God, the Precious Treasure, in My Daily Life*.

One of the reasons for me to write this book and choose this particular topic is because I see how important it is for us, the people of God, to see God's presence in our daily life. Knowing God to be by our side can make a big difference in how we would handle various situations day after day. We can become scared and overwhelmed easily if we do not think someone is always there to guide and protect us. Or we might feel alone and abandoned if we do not see anyone is around to help and comfort us.

As we can see, our world is increasingly in turmoil and filled with rage and violence. Additionally, technology and material things have slowly moved us away from our loving God and isolated us from being a caring neighbor for one another. But worldly things will not bring us peace and comfort, or turn us into a caring neighbor. If our world realizes that God is in its midst, it would definitely learn to behave better and treat others with love and respect, for God would hold it accountable for its actions. In some way, I believe the increasing violence and senseless shootings in our world correspond with the diminishing role of God in our lives. If we do not believe God is among us to hold us accountable and make us do the right things, then we would do anything we like, including things that might harm our neighbors, for some of us like to push the boundary to see how far we can get away with our misdeeds.

Although our world might be cynical and indifferent about God, many of us still appreciate the role of God and religion in our lives and continue to search for God's presence around us. As an experienced priest, I have seen many of us who have searched for various ways every day to be close to God, whether it is in prayer or in acts of charity. We all want to fill our daily life with God's presence. We believe that by having God before us and behind us and all around us, we will not go astray or be tempted to do something wrong easily, for God will be there to help us stay on the right path. Furthermore, we might face lots of challenges in our lives, but we will not feel overwhelmed or discouraged if we know God is close to us, for God will give us strength and courage to deal with those challenges. God is truly the precious treasure you will be lucky to find.

Those are some of the reasons for me to write this book to give us, the people of God, a good source of encouragement and guidance on our journey of faith. This book attempts to show us how to find God's presence through the ebbs and flows of our daily and weekly life. It also helps us to have the right attitude and good vision to recognize God's presence, even in the toughest situations. That attitude and vision calls us to look at things as a glass half-full and have a complete trust in God. By having that attitude and vision, we can manage to deal with all kinds of situations in our lives, for we know what God would want us to do in a particular situation. We have nothing to fear or worry about, because God is always next to us to guide and support us. I pray that we would carry this book with us at all times and find it a wonderful source of guidance and comfort in our daily life.

Fr. Peter G. Vu

CHAPTER 1

WHY WE NEED GOD EVERY MOMENT OF OUR LIFE; SEVEN SIGNS TO SHOW THAT WE TRULY HAVE MET GOD: LOVE, MERCY, PEACE, JOY, HOPE, GENEROSITY, AND FAITHFULNESS

For us, the faithful, the question above should not come as a surprise, and we can cite all sorts of reasons to have God in our lives. Nonbelievers might debate back and forth on why they might need God in their lives. But we, the faithful, know beyond a shadow of a doubt the importance of God in our world. We believe God created the universe and continues to sustain it. Without God's continuous support, it would not be able to stand on its own. Everything would turn chaotic, and the whole world would fall apart. Nations would start wars with their neighbors, while natural disasters would happen all over the globe. The rich and the powerful would exploit the poor and the weak if God was not around to impose order and consequences for our actions. We might say God was the town sheriff that a town like our world would desperately need to maintain its peace and order.

Many of the faithful in the biblical times believed that God would punish bad people and reward the good ones in this time and the next. There are many examples in the Bible to support this belief, and we will examine this further in the later chapters. As someone who gives out rewards and punishments, God plays an important role of enforcing justice and holding all creatures accountable for their actions. Without God's presence, our world would turn chaotic and become lawless.

But we need God to do more than just maintain law and order. We need God to give us a sense of self-worth as we keep on living our life to the fullest with the blessing of a new day. We live in a world that is more interested in material things than spiritual matters. Therefore, it often neglects to nurture the spiritual life of the people and causes them to suffer all sorts of mental and psychological problems. The most serious problem is the mental illness that could cause a person to become suicidal and commit violent acts toward people around him or her. If there is a pandemic that has caused thousands of untimely deaths and tremendous pain, it would be the increasing number of suicides. Each year, there are about 45,000 recorded suicides, according to the Centers for Disease Control (CDC) and the National Center for Health Statistics (NCHS). On average, the annual US suicide rate increased 24 percent between 1999 and 2016. There are 123 suicides per day, and suicide is the tenth leading cause of death in the United States, according to the American Foundation for Suicide Prevention.

This trend clearly raises lots of concerns for our country and the whole of humanity. Unfortunately, there is no medication or modern treatment to prevent and cure this horrible phenomenon. The best way to tamp it down and reduce the number of suicides is to ask for divine help and surround our world with a divine presence. So far, most of the earthly solutions have not solved our suicide epidemic. For this problem is in fact closely related to spiritual health. We need to call on God to heal and nourish our spirit.

When a person takes his or her life, he or she hits a dead end and wants to give up on living. His or her spirit is troubled, and it causes a person to have a dismal outlook on life. He or she feels overwhelmed and does not know where to turn for help. Jesus knew how these troubled souls felt and often reached out to comfort and heal them during his ministry. He referred to them as "possessed" or "taken over by evil spirits." They were tortured spiritually and miserable in their daily life. Some of them could not live in a human community and found themselves being isolated and having to live among the tombs and the dead.

We learn in the Gospels that they could not find any help from anyone on Earth, except a divine figure like Jesus, who apparently could bring them out of their current state of mind and give them new spirit. He certainly brought them back from the dead and blessed them with a new life. That is the greatest blessing and wonderful miracle that God could bring to a troubled soul and possibly the suicide epidemic that our world is suffering now. That is why many people, especially the afflicted, have sought out Jesus for healing or done everything possible to stay close to the Lord. If we follow their example and search for God, the precious treasure, in our daily life, imagine all the blessings and miracles we might experience.

A lesser form of hopelessness that our world is suffering from a lot these days is depression. Thousands of people have suffered with this terrible illness and relied on medication and other earthly treatments to deal with it. Unfortunately, many people continue to endure this awful spiritual state and get stuck in the valley of darkness and hopelessness. They feel hopeless and overwhelmed by life's burden. They do not see the purpose and joy of their lives. Every day, they feel sad and do not seem to be motivated to do anything.

That is why we, the believers, rely on God and religion to give meaning to our lives and motivate us to go out and change the world. We love to engage with the world and find each day as an opportunity to carry out the mission of salvation that our faith has called us to do. Our faith and religion challenge us to bring the good news to the world and make a difference for it. As Christians, we are called to imitate the holy life of Jesus in this life so that we may be rewarded with the eternal life in the kingdom of Heaven. If there is one thing we Christians do not lack, it is hope. We Christians are hopeful people who always rely on divine power to help us deal with our life challenges and have courage to carry our daily crosses. We would do anything to stay close to God or find God's presence in our life. God will inspire and motivate us to be faithful witnesses of God's love to the world.

Suicide and depression are not the only problems people have to face these days. Another serious problem that many people of our time are suffering from is some form of addiction. People might be addicted to alcohol, drugs, other substances, pleasure, sex, gambling, food, and so on. They become a slave to those bad habits and commit terrible acts to satisfy their dark desires. They get stuck in that dark and self-destructive world and cannot find their way out. They need a guide and savior to set them free from their bad habits and dark desires, as Moses did for the people of God from their bondage of slavery in Egypt. The one who was there with Moses and knew how to do that was God. God can help them put an end to their addiction and begin a new life. God can guide them home from their wayward lifestyle. God can give them grace and strength to resist relapse and overcome their personal demons. Those demons often give empty promises and fading joy. The pleasure and gratification they promise usually do not last. Worse yet, all the troubles and pains hidden behind an addition would soon reappear.

Only God can take away our pains and help us deal with our troubles. True joy can only be found in God and nowhere else in this world. God will satisfy all of our needs and desires, and fill in wherever we might be lacking. That is why people of God have come to God since the beginning of creation and asked for what they have needed. God, in turn, has healed them and answered their needs according to God's time.

Besides addiction, many people these days also suffer from another silent killer: namely, loneliness. People who suffer from this illness feel isolated and abandoned. Everyone around them seems to care about no one else but themselves. No one cares enough to befriend a lonesome person. Our fast-paced society and busy lifestyle exacerbates this problem. People would rather hide behind a mobile phone or a computer to handle their daily tasks. They no longer enjoy interacting with other people face-to-face or see any benefit from it. Many people these days do not even talk to or know their neighbors. Community-gathering places like churches, temples, mosques, outdoor markets, malls, museums, libraries, and so on are no longer favorite places for people of our time. Caring for the elderly and nursing home visits are not the qualities that our current culture desires and promotes. We see our high-tech culture and comfortable lifestyle isolate us more, instead of improving our relationships and moving us closer to our neighbors. This causes many people to suffer loneliness and creates that deadly problem for our time. In fact, most people who committed violent acts and horrible killings so far were reported to be loners according to News reports.

Our modern medicine and other advanced treatments have not cured people from their feeling of loneliness. The only one who can bring comfort and companionship to a lonesome person is God, for God knows how to lift up our spirit by sending us some comforting and hopeful signs. God has all the right tools to cheer us and help us with our unique problems, if we know how to search for God. A lonesome person would not feel that way if he or she had God as his or her companion. That is why we, the faithful, go to church regularly or keep a daily prayer routine to keep ourselves in the presence of God all the time. We rarely feel lonely, because God is always by our side to keep us company.

Some people are afraid of being alone and would rush into a married relationship without much preparation or knowing their spouses well. That is why over half of our current marriages end up in divorce according to Pew Research Center. This divorce phenomenon has put lots of stress and pain on many individuals and the family institution in modern times. The cause of many violent acts happening in our country and around the world has often been a nasty divorce or a horribly broken relationship. Those vile acts have been about anger, jealousy, and vengeance. If God is around, God will dissuade or talk those culprits out of it. God would also want all married couples to remain in love and peace instead of getting separated and angry with each other. Nothing would bring tears and pain to God more than seeing a broken family, for God desires unity and peace. Imagine this: If the relationships of the three persons within the Godhead—the Holy Trinity—fell apart, God would cease to exist. God certainly sympathizes with a broken relationship and would do anything to heal it. When God is present in a relationship, chances are it would remain intact. Therefore, we should search for God in a married relationship and make God the center of it.

However, relationships are not the only problem we have to deal with each day. We also have to face health and resource problems. Some of us might have trouble with our health, while others struggle with getting enough basic necessities for their daily life. Our health issues could make our daily life miserable. Our lack of food, clothes, and decent housing might be due to a poor economic condition or bad employment. Many people in Jesus's time had to deal with similar problems and came to Jesus for help. They called on him to heal their leprosy, blindness, hearing problem, speech impediment, paralysis, and possession by evil spirits. They also asked him to feed and nourish them.

Jesus always responded to their needs and delivered them from their health problems. He did not want them to suffer a minute longer. He wished them to return to their normal self. Similarly, he felt sorry for the poor and the hungry. A hungry crowd kept looking for him, and he asked his disciples to feed them. Many of us also feel inadequate and lack all sorts of things in this life, including good health. We need to learn from the people of God and try to search for God like they did for their needs back then. We must have God by our side daily so that God can give us a helping hand in times of need. God can help take care of our health and heal us in body, mind, and spirit. Or, if we need help with basic necessities, God could lend us a helping hand and provide us with those things as well. When we are in the presence of God, lots of wonderful things will happen.

In case we cannot see the benefits of having God in our life yet, we need to take a look at this Biblical passage: "The Kingdom of heaven is like treasure hidden in a field. When a man found it, he hid it again, and then in his joy went and sold all he had and bought that field. Again, the Kingdom of heaven is like a merchant looking for fine pearls. When he found one of great value, he went away and sold everything he had and bought it" (Matthew 13:44–46). For us, the faithful, God and the Kingdom of Heaven are like the hidden treasure or the fine pearls. God is the source of true peace and happiness. If we can have a taste of it, it would be like being in Heaven. We would not want anything else. We would trade everything in this life for it. People have searched all over the world over the years for a peaceful and happy life. They have thought if they could get more money or material possessions, it might bring them a peaceful and happy life. But history has shown us that money or all the possessions are usually the source of evil and have brought misery and doom to their owners instead. Similarly, people have assumed that power, glamor, or pleasure might guarantee them a satisfied and joyful life. Unfortunately, most people associated with that often ended up being unhappy or terribly hurt.

The only way we could truly have a peaceful and happy life is to have God with us at all times, for God is the source of true peace and happiness. We do not have to rely on any form of alcohol, drugs, or other substances to achieve that. God can bring joy to our hearts and keep our lives peaceful amidst the chaos of the earthly world. God holds the key to our happy life on Earth and the eternal one in Heaven also. If we have God with us, we certainly have everything. We have nothing to worry or feel fearful about in this life. Like a motivated merchant, we strive every day to search for the precious treasure or fine pearls in God and would be willing to exchange everything we have for it. Once we have it, nothing else matters in this life. Therefore, in this book, we will figure out how to meet God every day and keep us close to God, for great and wonderful things happen when God is mixed with us!

One of the things we hear regularly from common folks and our political leaders is that they "have prayerfully considered" something, or they tell us that they "will pray for" someone or something, or they ask us to pray when our nation faces some natural disaster or catastrophe. But their lives and actions do not show that they really believe in prayer and the spiritual world. There is actually a disconnection between what they say publically and what they truly believe in their hearts. To put it another way, is the phrase "You are in my thoughts and prayers" simply a nice expression in our daily conversation, like other typical expressions (e.g., "Godspeed" or "God bless you")? Do people really mean all the spiritual things when they talk about them? Do people truly have a good connection with God and want us to have the same divine experience like they do? Or do they simply pretend to use the spiritual language to score political points and get good public approval?

What bothers me a lot is that we sometimes do not mean what we say in our conversations. Our actions do not match our words. We are still angry and hold grudges when we say, "I forgive you, and I will pray for you." Like our politicians, we can be pretentious and use religion for our own benefits and ambition. The scribes and Pharisees used to do that. Their abuse of religion and pretention of being pious made Jesus frown on them and call them hypocrites. Their real relationship with God did not match with their exterior piety. We learn that the scribes and Pharisees did not represent the real presence of God, but Jesus did in the eyes of the Gospel witnesses. There were many signs the people of God saw in Jesus to let them know the presence of God, besides his ability to do miracles and wonders. Those signs were love, mercy, peace, joy, hope, generosity, and faithfulness. In fact, they often said these things about Jesus: "We have never seen anything like this before," or "He taught us with such authority and not like our religious leaders," or "See how merciful and forgiving he was to him or her?"

Jesus showed us how important it is to have God around us and the big difference God would make in our lives. Miracles and wonderful things would happen when we were in the presence of God. Temptations and evil spirits certainly will not succeed when God is around us. We can see how valuable it is to surround ourselves with the presence of God. Realizing the blessing of God in our lives, I have intended to write this book and explore how we can tell if God is really present with us or not. As I mentioned above, religious and political leaders have often invoked God to support their causes or back up their arguments. But I have found that their actions often do not match their language of faith, or their way of life often does not reflect the presence of God. God and religion have become a political football for these leaders to use publically and cover up their real selves. It is difficult for us to see the presence of God around them when they do not live up to God's commandments and act on those. Similarly, ordinary people have used the language of faith to describe how God has changed them or to claim that they have God on their side. Sadly, their actions do not back up their rhetoric but further confuse the public, as they show all sorts of anger and hatred in everything they do.

In this book, I will lay out seven values that people have experienced in the presence of God and later shared with the world in our human history. Again, those are love, mercy, peace, joy, hope, generosity, and faithfulness. I will examine each one of those values to help us see why it is a real indication of the presence of God. Then I will put those values to a test as we review the stories of the Old and New Testaments in the Bible that reported the presence of God to see if that is true. All seven values do not have to be present in every single Bible story. But if we can find the trace of some of them in those stories, then we can trust those as good indicators to test future stories. By relying on these values, we can screen out any false or fake claim of divine presence and judge for ourselves if someone has truly experienced God's presence or not.

Next, we will use these values to see how they can help us find God in modern times. It is surely difficult for anyone of us to search for the presence of God in our secular and materialistic world. But I believe that if we search diligently and can count on those seven values to magnify the presence of God, we will find God anywhere, anytime in our present world. Later on, we will apply those values to a typical weekly life of an ordinary Christian and see how we can meet God in our daily routines. I pray that regular people like us can meet God and have a divine experience much easier throughout the week with the help of the seven values. Our day will go by faster, and our week will be more meaningful when we know that God is always near us.

Finally, we want to apply those values to some difficult and extraordinary situations, and see how they can help us experience the presence of God even in the darkest moments of our lives. If we cannot find God in those tough situations, we can use those values as ways to invite God to come to our aid and be with us in the extraordinary times, for we really need God in those difficult moments. We feel alone and overwhelmed in times of trial. We wonder where God has been for us and whether God might have forgotten about us. We think we might have faced a dead end and our world is closing in on us. All we want to do in those dark moments is to give up and get out of this messy world. However, there is still one more thing for us to do: We can welcome God to be a part of our struggle and difficult situation to give us a helping hand. With God by our side, we can deal with any tough situation and make it through unscathed, for God will deliver us from all danger and bring us good resolutions in the end. While waiting for God to complete the work for us in our times of trial, perhaps we can pray for peace and healing. God can also bring us comfort and hope in those difficult moments. It is always good for us to be in the presence of God.

We now go through the seven values and see how they can show us the presence of God. As indicators of divine presence, we can be assured that God will be found whenever we see those values.

The first value to indicate for us the presence of God is *love*. Here is how John the evangelist defines God in his letter: "Beloved, let us love one another, because love is of God; everyone who loves is begotten by God and knows God. Whoever is without love does not know God, for God is love. … No one has ever seen God. Yet, if we love one another, God remains in us, and his love is brought to perfection in us … God is love, and whoever remains in love remains in God and God in him" (1 John 4:7–16).

John connects love with God and tells us that love comes from God. Over the centuries, people have defined God as the Creator, the white-haired old man, the almighty judge, the source of life, the powerful spirit, and so on. But no one has ever talked about God as love. John was the first one who expanded our view of God and helped us connect with God at the basic human level: namely, love. Anyone who demonstrates any sign of love knows God and comes from God. If we remain in love and show acts of love to others, God is truly present with us and in our world. We might have never seen God, but if we live in love, we definitely have seen God, for God is love and the source of life for us.

Love can be found wherever we see caring, kindness, concern, respect, and sacrifice. When we see a married couple show their tenderness and respect for each other over the years, love is there and so is God. That love might be separated by distance or physical location, but it remains strong and unfading. When parents make sacrifices and stay committed to their families, we can see true love and the presence of God in their midst and home.

There was a young mother, Mary, who lost her husband to cancer. His death left her devastated and bewildered about the future of her family. She had to raise her young family on her own. She must have wondered where God was in her life or whether God still loved her. But that tragedy did not cripple her or render her paralyzed in her desire to live. Amazingly, she did not give up on living or let that tragedy make her bitter and angry at God. She continued to attend her home church and sent her two sons through parochial school with the support of her family and friends. She had to work two jobs while attending all the sports and school events for her children. Her love and sacrifice for her family is not only commendable but also a sign of the presence of God in our world. Sometimes, we let tragedies and the challenges of our lives prevent us from seeing God in our world. This young mother helps us recognize the presence of God by the love and sacrifices she made for her family. We can see God present in her family because of what she did for them. Her love and care for them is the sign of God's presence in our midst.

Similarly, whenever children or grandchildren take care of their elderly parents or grandparents, their love and respect for an older generation is apparent, and God is surely present among them. It is tough to find people who have concerns for the elderly and dare to care for them at home or a nursing home in our time. People seem to neglect the elderly and consider a nursing home as a place of leprosy. They drop off their elderly there and do not come back to visit them regularly after that. But there was a young man, Matt, who struggled to commit his father to a nursing home for veterans and tried to come back to visit him almost every week. He did not want to send his father away from home, and yet he had no choice because his father needed a lot of care. Matt also had his own family to look after. But he went to visit his father regularly while wondering if he had made the right decision for him. He saw his father's dementia get worse over time to the point of not recognizing Matt as his son. His father's outbursts also took him by surprise at his visits and sometimes made him cry. However, that never kept Matt from visiting his father at the nursing home every week. His concern and respect for his father brought God's presence to their midst. His love for his father is certainly a good indicator of the presence of God. It helps us see God present in a tough situation (like his father's). Whenever we see love and concern like that in our world, God is surely present there.

But God is more than love; God is merciful and forgiving. Wherever we see *mercy*, we will certainly find God. Luke the evangelist calls us to be different from the world and learn to love our enemies as our God does:

If you love those who love you, what credit is that to you? Even "sinners" love those who love them. And if you do good to those who are good to you, what credit is that to you? Even "sinners" do that. … But, love your enemies, do good to them, and lend them without expecting to get anything back. Then your reward will be great, and you will be sons and daughters of the Most High, because he is kind to the ungrateful and wicked. Be merciful, just as your Father is merciful. Do not judge, and you will not be judged. Do not condemn, and you will not be condemned. Forgive, and you will be forgiven. (Luke 6:32–37)

> We are asked to imitate God the Father and learn to be merciful and forgiving. Jesus's entire

ministry was about calling people from their sinful way of life and showing them God's mercy and forgiveness. In fact, many of Jesus's parables for the people of God were about how merciful and forgiving our God is.

One of the famous parables about God's mercy and forgiveness is the one of the prodigal son. In that parable, the youngest son squandered his father's gifts to him and offended his father in many ways by his sinful lifestyle. Thankfully, he looked over his sinful past and realized he needed to change. He had a moment of conversion and decided to come home to ask his father for mercy and forgiveness. He found all of that and much more from his compassionate father. Indeed, all the conversion stories in our Christian tradition are true because they have God's mercy and presence in their storyline. To put it another way, the reason we can see the presence of God throughout the Bible is because it is full of God's mercy and conversion stories. So wherever we find God's mercy in the conversion stories, we will certainly see the presence of God.

We surely can name many examples that involve mercy in our lives. But here we will try to find out how God can be present in those cases. For now, let me share with you two of my own examples and show you how I saw God present in those situations. The first example comes from a young boy, Jim, who apparently was bullied by a group of older kids in his high school. They made fun of his clothes, called him names, shoved him around at recess, and harassed him every chance they got. The boy was all shook up and not interested in going to school anymore. He made up one excuse after another to stay home. His teachers were concerned about the number of his school absences, while his parents wondered about his emotional and mental well-being. He seemed quiet and moody. He spent more time by himself and tried to figure out how to get back at those bullies. He thought about taking the law into his own hands and gunning them down like the lawless Wild West. After all, school laws and their enforcers did not do anything with the school bullies or keep them from taunting other kids. As this young man tried to come up with a plan to carry out his vengeance, he had an epiphany about his evil act and was challenged by his Lord Jesus to turn the other cheek and show mercy to his torturers. He was not quite sure what happened in that brief moment of epiphany, but he might have had a divine encounter. That encounter had not only shown him the presence of God in our world but also transformed his thoughts of vengeance. After some prayerful consideration, he changed his mind about hurting his enemies and put an end to his violent act. His act of mercy to people who had hurt him brought God back into his life, and in turn, God helped him figure out better ways to deal with those school bullies. Because of his act of mercy, we can see the real presence of God in our world and experience a wonderful miracle of transformation in this young man.

Another example that would connect our acts of mercy with the presence of God in our world can be seen when the family of a victim can forgive their accuser. There was a murder case in which the alleged murderer was put on trial and convicted for killing his victim, Sue. After the trial, the family of the poor victim—while drowning in tears and grief—was able to state publically that they had forgiven the accused. Their merciful and forgiving statement shocked everyone and helped the whole community begin its healing process. This special family and their forgiving act is difficult for us to find in our dog-eat-dog world. We often hear the victim's loved ones express their hurt, outrage, and condemnation of the accused. It is quite rare for us to see the family of a victim express mercy and forgiveness to someone who hurt and inflicted pain on them and their loved one. The only one who expressed mercy and forgiveness regularly, even on the Cross, was our Lord Jesus. We know God was always with him, especially when he showed mercy and forgave repentant sinners. Therefore, whenever we see or express mercy and forgiveness, God must be there. On the contrary, whenever we judge and condemn people, we wrongfully assume the role of God and push God far away from our world.

However, *mercy* is not the only indicator of the presence of God. Another sign to point us to God is *peace*. John the evangelist describes the link between God and peace as follows: "'This makes us [Jesus's disciples] believe that you [Jesus] came from God.' … Jesus answered, 'A time is coming, and has come, when you will be scattered, each to his own home. … I have told you these things, so that in me you may have peace. In this world, you will have trouble. But, take heart! I have overcome the world'" (John 16:30–33).

Jesus wants to tell us that we will definitely run into troubles in this world. We will have to face all sorts of problems and difficulties each day. But don't worry. Let's have faith in Jesus and come to him to find peace for ourselves, for true peace can only be found in God and not in this world.

Besides love, peace is another blessing we desire in real life, for everything around us is often chaotic and difficult. Nothing usually happens the way we want. Our daily life is typically full of surprises. Most of us want to buy a home in a quiet neighborhood or look forward to our vacations to find some peaceful rest. In addition to our daily chaos, many of us sometimes get jealous and begin to create fights with one another. It is not surprising that we usually have a tough time finding God in our chaotic life. We have a better chance of encountering God in a peaceful setting like a church, temple, mosque, or retreat than in the world. Most people in the Bible and real life usually have a divine encounter when they are in a quiet, peaceful environment. God cannot be found when there is violence, fighting, or war. If we want to meet God in this life, we must search for a peaceful setting or create a peaceful environment for prayer time in our daily life.

We all have a busy daily schedule and live a fast-pace life. Our life is full of pressure and tension. Every day, we try to maintain peace and keep things under control around us. We admire people like Annie—a divorced, single parent who has to raise a young family on her own. Every morning she has to pack lunches and get her three young children to school. She also keeps a forty-hour workweek and does her best to do everything around home, such as cooking, cleaning, doing laundry, cutting grass, and shoveling snow. She lets her children participate in sports, music, and other extracurricular activities. She tries hard not to miss any school event or her children's activities. On the weekend, she gets her children to participate in Sunday school at her home church and does grocery shopping for them. Although she does not have much free time, she believes in paying forward for God's blessings on her family and tries to volunteer for her church and her children's school. If Annie's busy lifestyle was not challenging enough to cause her blood pressure to rise and make her uptight, she has to deal with bad drivers on the road and mean people at work every day.

But she never let life pressures and other outside factors rattle her. She always has the peace of Christ in her heart and tries to maintain that sense of peace in her home and around her. She is grounded in peace by keeping a good relationship with her God—the true source of peace—in prayer. She remembers that the one thing Jesus wants his disciples to have after the wonderful news of his resurrection is peace. He often greeted them with "Peace be with you." She did not understand why peace was so essential in her daily life until now. To put it another way, she has met the risen Christ—God—like the early disciples did and found true peace to help her deal with all the chaos in her life and around her. The peace she has experienced in her soul shows us that God is present in her life. That divine presence has given her confidence and strength to deal with her life changes and maintain a loving, peaceful home for her family.

The presence of God brings peace to not only a busy mother like Annie but also two fighting neighbors. Joe has been living in this old neighborhood for a few decades and recently has seen a new family move next door. At first, the new neighbor would just let their dogs run loose and go across Joe's neatly cut lawn to pee and trample on his beautiful flower bed. It seemed like every weekend in the summer, the new neighbor would have a party that created a traffic jam and woke up everyone late at night with loud music in this quiet neighborhood. This whole circus went on for the entire summer and made the simmering hot season a bit unbearable for Joe. But he tried to be patient and not to get mad at his new neighbor yet. When a summer storm knocked down a number of branches, the new neighbor simply picked them up and tossed them across to Joe's yard. Again, Joe was tempted to go over and let the new neighbor know his frustration. He might have even declared war with the new neighbor.

Then he thought that autumn—a new season—might turn over a new leaf and all these uneasy feelings between two neighbors would quickly disappear. After all, Joe has always been a peaceful man and tried to avoid conflicts if possible. The beautiful fall season finally arrives and calls on all the trees to shed their leaves. Unfortunately, the new neighbor has not imitated the trees and shed his obnoxious behaviors. Soon, the yard is covered with thousands of dead leaves. The new neighbor continues his bad behaviors and blows all the leaves over to Joe's yard. Joe is speechless when he sees how messy his yard looks compared to his neighbor's remarkably clean one. He has put up with this inconsiderate and selfish neighbor for almost half a year and cannot hold back his anger and contempt anymore. He wants to unleash his fury and declare war on the new neighbor.

But Joe thinks about the upcoming holidays and Christmas season, with its message of peace on Earth and goodwill toward mankind. That message is what brought Jesus, the son of God, into our world and exactly what Joe wants the world to experience and share with one another. He does not want war and fighting with his new neighbor. He feels that he needs to be the ambassador of peace and goodwill toward mankind, like Jesus once was at Christmas. He needs to hold back his anger and frustration toward his new neighbor. The moment Joe embraces peace and goodwill, instead of anger and frustration, is when he meets God. That epiphany moment is when God transforms him and opens his heart to a new solution for his problem with his new neighbor. His willingness to embrace peace opens him up to have an encounter with God.

However, a peaceful attitude is not the only indicator and pathway to the presence of God. *Joy* is another way to connect us to God. In the Bible and real life, we learn that people who have seen the Lord are usually full of joy. Their appearance would be the first thing that experience changes, before their attitude and lifestyle would follow. Moses was one of the blessed people who were able to meet the Lord face-to-face on Mount Sinai. After that meeting, his appearance changed and was described as follows: "When Moses came down from Mount Sinai with two tablets of the Testimony in his hands, he was not aware that his face was radiant because he had spoken with the Lord. When Aaron and all the Israelites saw Moses, his face was radiant" (Exodus 34:29–35). However, the presence of God did not change only his appearance but also his trust and commitment to the Lord. He would joyfully do anything for the Lord and know that the Lord would help him complete it.

Other people in the Bible—like the three disciples Peter, James, and John, who apparently had a divine encounter on Mount Tabor—also experienced similar changes like Moses did. Their experience was recounted as follows: "After six days, Jesus took with him Peter, James, and John the brother of James, and led them up a high mountain by themselves. There he was transfigured before them. His face shone like the sun, and his clothes became as white as the light. … Peter said to Jesus, 'Lord, it is good for us to be here. If you wish, I will put up three shelters—one for you, one for Moses, and one for Elijah.'… And a voice from the cloud said, 'This is my son, whom I love, with him I am well pleased. Listen to him'" (Matthew 17:1–6). The three disciples were not the only ones who were joyful and experienced a personal transformation but also Jesus. His appearance evidently was changed upon his meeting with God, the Father. That is what the presence of God would do to a person.

Another example in the Bible to show us the joy and change in a person upon being in the presence of the Lord is the appearance of the risen Christ to the fearful disciples. This is how they reacted to that appearance: "When the disciples were together, with the doors locked for fear of the Jews, Jesus came and stood among them and said, 'Peace be with you!' After he had said this, he showed them his hands and side. The disciples were overjoyed when they saw the Lord" (John 20:19–20). That is how the early disciples felt upon a divine encounter. Other divine apparitions in modern times share the same reaction of the lucky witnesses.

They all feel joyful and report other personal changes after those divine encounters. The joy of their divine encounters compels them to go out and tell it to the whole world.

One of the joyful events many couples celebrate in their experienced relationship is a wedding. After a period of being friends and getting to know one another, a couple takes the next step in their friendship to commit themselves to each other for life. This one particular couple, Carlos and Louisa, has had to face lots of hardships during their courtship. They both came to this country as immigrants and have dealt with the politics of immigration, the language and cultural difficulties, and the lack of resources. But they worked hard to build their new lives in America. They have to take low-paying jobs and go to school while working full-time. Life challenges cannot intimidate them or diverge them from achieving their lifelong goals. Their first goal is to be able to get married and commit their lives to each other in a church amidst their families and friends. They rejoice on this special day and feel as if it is a small miracle that God has done for them. Their joy on their wedding day reminds us of the presence of God in their midst on that special day and throughout their lives. God certainly blesses their marriage union and continues to watch over their new family. Like the wedding in Cana, they have invited Jesus to their wedding by having it in a church and know that he will help them in a time of need. God is indeed present at their wedding and makes their joy complete.

Another example to show us the presence of God in a joyful occasion is the birth and baptism of a child. Most married couples do not have any problem with getting pregnant and beginning their new family together. Unfortunately, there are some couples who suffer the devastating fate of sterile couples in the Bible and cannot have children. They feel God has punished them or abandoned them. They do not know why they cannot create a new family and would be willing to try anything to have a baby. One young couple has tried to get pregnant for several years after their wedding but has not succeeded. They keep coming to God in prayer for months and ask for a miracle. Their prayer is finally answered when they learn that the wife is pregnant. They rejoice and thank God for the miracle. Soon, they are able to welcome the birth of a healthy baby boy, Paul. Their joy is apparent as they dedicate their bundle of joy to God with the ritual of baptism in their home church. God is certainly present at the baptismal celebration. Indeed, they met God the moment they found joy again in their life as they received the miraculous news of pregnancy. Their joy is surely a sign of the presence of God in our world. That divine presence is confirmed by a miracle God has done for this barren couple.

In addition to *joy*, *hope* is another indicator of the presence of God in our world. The prophet Jeremiah helps us see how we can find God through hope: "'For I [the Lord] know the plans I have for you,' declares the Lord, 'plans to prosper you and not to harm you, plans to give you hope and a future. Then you will call upon me and come and pray to me, and I will listen to you. You will seek me and find me when you seek me with all your heart, I will be found by you'" (Jeremiah 29:11–14). Jeremiah reminds us that the Lord has plans for all of us. He is our true hope, and we can count on him for anything, even in desperate times. Whenever we dare to reach for some inspiring and hopeful thoughts in our challenging times, we will meet God and experience the divine power. For where there is hope, there will we find God.

From the moment of being kicked out of the Garden of Eden, we humans were condemned to a life of toil and sweat to earn a living. Nothing we do in this life will come easy for us. Sometimes, life pressures or an evil act can overwhelm and scare us—just ask the survivors of a war, a terminal illness, or an abusive relationship, and we will see what it takes for them to overcome that scary and dead-end situation. It takes hope and divine help to give them a reason to wake up every day and continue living. Otherwise, they will not see the purpose for their lives and then decide to give up on living or end their lives. That is the root cause of all suicide cases, which have become a pandemic in our modern society.

There is a young gal, Julia, who is shy and unpopular in her high school and not quite sure about what she will do in the future. Meanwhile, her older sister, Audrey, is determined to pursue a career in medicine, and her youngest brother, Steven, wants to go into business administration and make lots of money. She feels lost in this world, as life pressures and market competition continues to marginalize people like her. She does not know whom she can talk to about her problem or how to express her fear and anxiety about her future. The only thing she feels she can do is to take herself out of this miserable world and end her life. While her life is at the dead end, she finds a hopeful message at church one Sunday as her pastor reads this gospel passage: "Come to me all who are weary and find life burdensome and I will refresh you. Take my yoke upon your shoulder and learn from me for I am humble and gentle of heart. Your souls will find rest. For my yoke is easy and my burden light" (Matthew 11:28–30).

This young woman, who has been feeling down about her life, happened to be in church that day and found God in the form of a hopeful gospel message. The Lord asks her to put his yoke on her heavy shoulders so that he can lift her up and give her a fresh new life. That might sound counterintuitive. But, like being on a teeter-totter, she can feel uplifted only if she will counterbalance her heavily burdened life with the extra weight on the other side of this life journey. In this case, the weight on other side is the Lord. She thankfully found God that day and turned all her troubles and fear over to him. The Lord gave her relief and a fresh new life by showing her what she would do with her life. God restored hope in her life from the moment she heard God's voice in that gospel passage. Hope is indeed a sign of the presence of God. It gives birth to a new life, new possibilities, and countless miracles for a desperate person.

Here is another example to show us why hope is not only an indicator of the presence of God but also a reason for us to believe in miracles. A young father, Mike, is rushed to the local hospital for an unknown reason. He loses all strength and cannot move around. Worse yet, the hospital staff does not know what causes it and cannot issue any effective treatment to him. The only thing they can do for him for now is give him antibiotics intravenously. But even that seems to cause more problems than helping him. He begins to develop red rashes all over the place while his body swells up like a balloon. His doctors start to have doubts about their ability to treat him and ask his young family to come in to see him one last time and prepare for the worst. But his loved ones refuse to give up and decide to pray for a miracle. Some of the hospital staff do not think all of that praying will work. After almost two months in the hospital, his doctors have found out positively what is wrong with him. Somehow, he has contracted a flesh-eating disease and will need some aggressive treatment before it is too late. The hospital staff quickly carry out their treatment for him, and before long, he makes a complete recovery.

After this miraculous event, his family is able to convince many hospital staff to have faith in a higher power and become strong believers. They sure have had a divine encounter and known how to put their trust and hope in the Lord. Hope not only brings this family comfort and miracles in tough time but also helps them show the world the presence of God. Likewise, when we can find God's presence in our daily life, wonderful things will happen around us. We learn in the gospels that anytime God's people were around Jesus, they would be fed, healed, and able to experience all kinds of miracles. Therefore, they constantly searched for him and wanted to be around him. Our hope in God and the eternal life certainly brings us closer to Jesus and assures us his presence in our daily life.

We should not lose hope if we want to see God around us. However, there is another attribute we should have in our lives if we want to experience a divine encounter: namely, *generosity*. This attribute is one of the divine qualities. Throughout the Bible, God has shown his blessings and mercy generously to the people of God. If the creation of the world is the first exhibit of the divine generosity, God has succeeded in doing that. Like an endless source of spring water, God has generously shown his people one blessing after another from day one. When Adam asked God to bless him with Eve, God did not hesitate to grant his prayer request after already giving him the whole paradise-like garden. God continues to watch over the first family and people of God by pouring down on them many blessings every day. God also pardons their sins and generously extends his mercy on them. God never lets the sun shine and the rain drop only on saintly people. God generously lets good things happen to both saints and sinners, and surprises the whole world. God sure hates sins but not sinners. God seems to act on the principle of generosity in all of his dealings with the world. The Bible has many stories to support that.

One of those stories is the parable of the workers in the vineyard. The owner goes out at various time of the day and hires workers for his vineyard. At the end of the workday, he summons them all for pay, beginning with the last-hired worker. He wants to give the last-hired worker the same pay as the first-hired one. His generosity causes the first-hired worker to feel that he is being treated unfairly. The owner of the vineyard responds as follows: "Friend, I am not being unfair to you. Didn't you agree to work for a denarius? Take your pay and go. I want to give the man who was hired last the same as I gave you. Don't I have the right to do what I want with my own money? Or, are you envious because I am generous?" (Matthew 20:1-16).

But God does not act generously alone. God also encourages the people of God to imitate his example and do the same. We have seen how Jesus commends people who dare to live generously in our world through the Biblical story of the widow's offering (Luke 21:1-4) or the parable of the Good Samaritan (Luke 10:25-37). When we live generously, God is there to praise and bless us. Another good example to highlight that message is the biblical story of the widow in Zarephath (1 Kings 17:10-16). Once, the whole region was hit by a severe drought, and the harvest was poor. The food supply was scarce. A widow and her only son were preparing their last meal together when a stranger named Prophet Elijah showed up at the door of their house, asking for something to eat and drink. Instead of refusing to share their little amount of food with this stranger and turning him away, they invited him to stay and eat whatever food they might have without worrying about tomorrow. Their generosity touched the heart of God, and God performed a miracle for them by not letting their jar of flour run low for a whole year. This miraculous story reminds us why we should act and live generously in our daily life. When we do that, God will reveal himself to us through a miracle and repay us abundantly.

One of the challenges for us in modern times is that we do not seem to meet God or experience a miracle often in our daily life. Unlike biblical people, who evidently experienced many divine encounters and saw lots of miracles in their lives, we feel distant from God and have a tough time finding miracles in our technological society. Besides, we see lots of selfish people and greedy acts being reported on the news. We find many people these days do not have a generous spirit or an open attitude to new possibilities. There is all sorts of fighting and bickering over many things. Everyone cannot work together and make compromises for the common good. God will never be found in this kind of environment. When we have a generous spirit and an open attitude to God's work in our lives, we will meet God easily and experience miracles often.

We all have met many generous people in our lives, and they certainly remind us of the presence of God in our midst. Here are a couple of examples of those for us to look over and see why they might help us experience God in this world. The first example is about a retiree named Bob. He has been working at a local company for over thirty years and recently decided to retire. But he does not want to stay home and do nothing. He wants to get more involved with his home church and local community. He is already an usher at his church but signs up to volunteer to paint some parish rooms, cut the church lawn, and drive the elderly to church and doctors' appointments. He also takes meals to the homebound and the poor. He likes to volunteer one day a week at the local soup kitchen. If there is any free time left, Bob comes to a nearby elementary school and reads to the children to encourage them to love books. His boundless energy and generous spirit fascinates everyone around him. His generosity touches strangers and changes many lives. Some people might not share his same faith, but his generous spirit has helped them meet his God. They begin to see how caring and kind his God is. They might not have met God before, but Bob's generous spirit has made God real for them.

Another example of generosity that we could highlight is the case of organ donation. After a tragic car accident, the family of the young victim, Janet, decides to donate her organs to save the lives of others. Most people would focus solely on themselves in a time of tragedy and grief like this. But this particular family has always taught its members to be generous and learn to share with others. In spite of its tough situation, this family never abandons its support of the important values, like generosity. This virtue has not only brought them comfort but also shown others the presence of God amidst tears and sadness. We might think it is tough to find God in a sad and tragic situation like this. But if we try to think and act generously, we will allow God to reveal himself all around us. On the contrary, if we are not generous in our thoughts and actions toward others, we would have a tough time experiencing God in our world, for God is generous by nature. Unfortunately, that is what is happening in our world these days. It is difficult to find God in our world, as everyone cannot think and act generously toward one another. Most people get stuck in their own beliefs or ideologies and have a tough time seeing the points of view of their neighbors. They are not open to let God show up in other ways. As a result of that, we see a lot more fights and bickering than we do God.

Finally, another indicator to help us experience the presence of God is *faithfulness*. Throughout the Bible, God demanded the people of God to be faithful to his commandments and rewarded those who lived up to them. The people of God were lured by other idols and had to face lots of challenges. What helped them overcome those temptations and challenges was to remain faithful to their God. By being faithful, they were able to rely on God for help and protection. God always answered their calls and came to their rescue in difficult times. Some of the faithful servants of God were Abraham, Moses, and King David. These people were so loyal to God that they seemed to have God by their side at all times, and their prayers were mostly answered as they wished. The Bible lets us know that God was present with God's faithful ones and happy to perform miracles for them. In fact, Jesus often required people to have faith if they wanted to see miracles. The Lord will not show up to perform miracles unless the people of God have faith.

Here is an exchange between Jesus and a woman who desired divine help and a miracle: "The woman came and knelt before him [Jesus]. 'Lord, help me!' she said. He replied, 'It is not right to take the children's bread and toss it to their dogs.' 'Yes, Lord,' she said, 'but even the dogs eat the crumbs that fall from their master's table.' Then Jesus answered, 'Woman, you have great faith! Your request is granted.' And her daughter was healed from that very hour" (Matthew 15:25-28). The woman put her faith in Jesus, and that helped her experience a miracle and the presence of God in her life. Her faith is difficult for us to find in our modern times. She was tested and put down but did not give up on believing in Jesus as the savior for her problem. Unfortunately, people nowadays do not search for God fervently and would find every excuse to abandon their faith. That is why it is tough for us to see miracles and experience the presence of God in our world these days.

However, there are people who live a life of faithfulness and can show us how they might meet God in their daily life. A married couple, Tim and Jan, who recently celebrated their sixty-fifth wedding anniversary, wants to share their life secrets with me and other newly married couples. Like most couples, they have had their differences and argued sometimes in the course of their marriage. But they have learned to compromise and forgive each other. That is how they could remain faithful to each other for that long. During those marriage years, they have often come to God for guidance and help on various things. Their faithfulness to each other has encouraged them to remain faithful to God.

God is able to carry out many miracles in their marriage and let them experience his blessings for their family. They believe that, without the presence of God in their marriage, they might not have made it this far. Their wedding anniversary is surely the result of the divine presence in our world. They could not have experienced that blessing unless they had committed to be faithful to each other for that long. Faithfulness is truly a good sign to show us the presence of God in our world.

Another example of faithfulness as a good indicator for the presence of God is the story of Emma and her dog, La Luz. Emma has had La Luz for a couple of years, and they have been inseparable. She feeds him, plays with him, talks to him, and takes him out for a walk every day. They have become best friends and shared lots of things together. Their faithful and enjoyable friendship has made a big difference in their lives. They would not be the same without this amazing, loyal friendship. They sure have made lots of sacrifices for this relationship. Their faithfulness to each other is a sign of the presence of God in their midst. We might not think God would have anything to do with the bond between a little girl and her dog. But God is present even in this relationship because they are loyal and kind to each other. Whenever we are faithful and committed to a relationship, God is there to guide and help us to continue on with it. We have to make sacrifices and work hard to maintain that relationship. We also need help from above to complete that task. It is difficult to sacrifice for someone unless we care and remain faithful to that person. But if we truly make sacrifices and stay focused on a relationship, we would certainly see God present in it.

CHAPTER 2

HOW GOD WAS FOUND IN THE OLD TESTAMENT

The mystery of God has fascinated our human mind and intrigued many scholars, just as the mystery of science has kept Albert Einstein and other scientists on their hunt for the truth about the universe over the years. Scholars and ordinary people have asked questions and searched the universe to figure out the identity of God. They have scanned the four corners of the earth to see if they can find any sign of God's presence, but God remains a mystery. Philosophers and theologians have gradually come up with many concepts and divine qualities to describe God. God is considered like a spirit or a form that cannot be touched or embraced by our human senses. Although we cannot see that spirit or form, it still has a great impact in real life and helps keep the whole creation alive. Without the spirit of God, every living thing would go out of existence.

Describing God as a spirit or form is a great step and a wonderful achievement for us humans to get to know God a little better. Still, it is hard for a human being to visualize and comprehend God. That is why theologians have begun to attach these attributes to God: all-powerful, almighty, omnipotent, omniscient, sacred, holy, eternal, and so on. Other future theologians have steadily added more divine qualities such as love, mercy, forgiveness, beauty, creating, peace, joy, happiness, kindness, caring, comforting, life-giving, just, fair, generous, patient, faithful, and so on. This updating process of the image of God continues as we humans try to solve the mystery of God. In this chapter, we will examine the Old Testament to learn how the people in this period identified God in their world.

In the book of Genesis, God appears as the source of life and creation, and yet remains a mystery. Here is how God is described: "In the beginning, when God created the heavens and the earth, the earth was a formless wasteland, and darkness covered the abyss, while a mighty wind swept over the waters" (Genesis 1:1-2). God–the original form–gives form and order to a "formless" and chaotic world. God provides an orderly structure and turns a dark, chaotic place to a bright, lively world. God said, "Let there be light, and there was light" (Genesis 1:3). God brightens up a place and wakes it up from its sleeping state. Then God said, "Let the water under the sky be gathered into a single basin, so that the dry land may appear. … Let the water teem with an abundance of living creatures, and on the earth let birds fly beneath the dome of the sky. … Let the earth bring forth all kinds of living creatures: cattle, creeping things, and wild animals of all kinds. … God created human in God's image" (Genesis 1:9, 20, 24, 27). God appears to create life and fills the whole of creation with living things. God seems to play the role of creating and generating life. God desires the whole creation to live and be fertile.

Many people in our time often think that God could only be found in church or a sacred place. But the first story of the Bible reminds us that God was very much a part of nature. God was intimately involved with the entire work of creation and helped make it a reality. Everything we see in nature has God's fingerprint on it.

God created sunlight, sky, sea, water, birds, fish, wild animals, plants, trees, flowers, fruits, and other things in nature. God wanted the whole creation to grow, produce, and prosper. The beauty and harmony we see in nature reflects God's qualities and ever-presence with us. Many people can connect easily with God through nature and find God's presence in it. They feel at peace and reenergized after a nature walk. In fact, more people nowadays identify God with nature instead with the building structure of a church. They want to be far removed from the busy city lifestyle and enjoy the peaceful, quiet way of life in the country. They certainly can find God easier in the country than in the urban environment.

However, God also tries to hold God's creatures accountable for their actions. God did not shy away from that role and forced the first human couple—Adam and Eve—out of the Garden of Eden for violating God's command and eating the forbidden fruits. God condemned them to a harsh life of sweat and toil. Similarly, God held Cain accountable for his murderous act toward his brother, Abel, and said, "What have you done? Listen, your brother's blood cries out to me from the soil. Therefore, you shall be banned from the soil that opened its mouth to receive your brother's blood from your hand. If you till the soil, it shall no longer give you its produce. You shall become a restless wanderer on the earth" (Genesis 4:15). God apparently switched from the role of creating and generating life at the moment of creation to the role of judging and punishing his creatures for their misdeeds. God finally came to this conclusion before releasing the deadly flood on the whole creation: "When God saw how corrupt the earth had become, since all mortals led depraved lives on earth, He said to Noah: 'I have decided to put an end to all mortals on earth; the earth is full of lawlessness because of them. So, I will destroy them and all life on earth" (Genesis 6:12–13).

The first couple met God when they were confronted about their misdeed and received their punishment for it. It must have been hard for them to see how angry and disappointed God was as they stood before him. They were blessed with a life of a royal couple and were told how to conduct themselves to deserve that way of life. Unfortunately, they did not listen well and did what they were not supposed to do. They ate the forbidden fruit and had to face the toughest punishment by losing all their privileges in the Garden of Eden. They were condemned to a life of hard labor and being far away from God. This encounter with God would often take place on Judgment Day, as everyone would receive rewards or punishments according to his or her conduct. But Adam and Eve met God and faced their judgment right here in this life. Their encounter with God was a bit unusual, but it carried great impact. It affected them for the rest of their lives and future generations.

Like them, their oldest son, Cain, had a similar encounter with God, as he had to face the consequence for his action. He apparently killed his younger brother, Abel, out of envy and jealousy. He did not like the fact that his brother received more blessings from God than he did. He had to destroy his competition, but God did not let him get away with that evil act. His punishment was worse than his parents'. All his hard work with the soil would not produce any good result, and he would have to wander the earth to search for food. His encounter with God must be unforgettable, as he received his punishment right here in this life. Yet God did not want the cycle of vengeance and killing to keep on happening. God tried to stop it and warned any retribution on Cain with grave consequence. Again, most people would not want to meet God under the circumstances like Cain or his parents did. Facing God for a judgment or a punishment is never fun. But in both cases, God remained hidden while handing out to them God's punishment right here on Earth. Some people might refer to the encounter with God by Cain and his parents (Adam and Eve) as the voice of conscience. After violating God's commands and doing something wrong, they were remorseful and tried to change their lives. This divine encounter is common and significant for most penitents. It helps bring closure to a difficult and painful situation.

God certainly did not hesitate to follow through with the punishment and wiped out the whole of creation with the epic Flood. Because of actions like that, God took on the image of a judge and law enforcer. God made sure the people of God would obey God's Commandments and, in turn, protected them from their enemies. God also looked out for their best interests and promised to lead them to the magnificent land where milk and honey would flow out of it. This covenant was made between God and Abraham—the leader of God's people—and passed on to his descendants. Abraham, his son (Isaac), and his grandson (Jacob) never wanted to let God down and continued to obey God's Commandments. They remained faithful to God and never broke any Commandment or followed another god. Abraham once played the role of an intercessor as he tried to ask God to spare the destruction of two cities, Sodom and Gomorrah, for their awful sins. If he could find ten innocent people in Sodom, he begged God not to destroy the city. In the end, he could not do it, and God had to carry out the severe punishment by raining down fire and burning it to the ground. Here, God appeared angry and judging as he carried out proper punishment for the sins of the people of God. Although that punishment was real and fully executed, God remained hidden.

However, the mystery of God continued to be revealed to Abraham throughout his life. God never stopped communicating to him and commanded him to follow God's laws and Jewish tradition. He never disobeyed God's commands or tried to test God's patience. Once, God attempted to test Abraham's faithfulness and called him to sacrifice his only beloved son, Isaac. Anyone else would have objected to God's command immediately. But Abraham did not and obediently followed through with God's command. As he was about to sacrifice his son, God stopped him and called him to offer the ram in place of his beloved child. Although God's identity remained hidden, this special encounter between Abraham and God gives us a glimpse of where God might reside. Here is how that encounter was reported: "Abraham named the site Yahweh-yireh ('the Lord will see'); hence people now say, 'On the mountain the Lord will see.' Again the Lord's messenger called to Abraham from heaven and said, 'I swear by myself, declares the Lord, that because you acted as you did[,] not withholding from me your beloved son, I will bless you abundantly and make your descendants as countless as the stars of the sky and the sands of the seashore'" (Genesis 22:14–17). God's creation looked a lot more secured and protected as God kept watched over it from the high mountain and the heavens above. Both places are lofty and far away from our mundane ground. Perhaps that explains why people often look up to Heaven when praying or having a conversation with God.

God remained close to Abraham's family and kept watch over his son, Isaac. God protected Isaac and guided him after the death of his father, Abraham. Isaac had his own family, with two children: Esau and Jacob. He eventually gave his special blessing on the younger son, Jacob, instead of the oldest son, Esau, as the Jewish tradition would dictate. That caused resentment and a fight between Abraham's two sons. Jacob went on the run to avoid his brother's wrath and ended up taking a rest overnight at a shrine in Bethel. While he slept, God's messengers appeared in his dream, along with a stairway reaching to the heavens, and told him, "Know that I am with you; I will protect you whenever you go, and bring you back to this land. I will never leave you until I have done what I promised you" (Genesis 28:15). Jacob evidently met God during his flight to avoid Esau. In his time of fear and danger, he found God for a brief moment and was given a message of comfort and reassurance. Still, God remained a mystery and could only be contacted in a dream.

Unlike many figures in the Old Testament, Jacob was so blessed to have his second divine encounter. While he was still on the run from his brother, Esau, Jacob had to spend a night in a tent and had a struggle with an angel all night long. That wrestling match was described as the following:

Some man wrestled with him [Jacob] until the break of dawn. When the man saw that he could not prevail over him, he struck Jacob's hip at its socket, so that the hip socket was wrenched as they wrestled. The man then said, "Let me go, for it is day break." But, Jacob said, "I will not let you go until you bless me." ... Then, the man said, "You shall no longer be spoken of as Jacob, but as Israel, because you have contended with divine and human beings and have prevailed." ... Jacob named the place Peniel, "because I have seen God face to face," he said, "yet my life has been spared." (Genesis 32:25–31)

Jacob had a real, physical encounter with the divine this time and had a broken limb to prove it. He must have felt extremely special to meet God twice and have a personal conversation with God. Most people would be lucky if they could personally meet God once. Jacob was blessed with two divine encounters. Yet God remained a mystery for him.

Jacob's openness to meet the Lord and his relentless search for God in his life encourages us to imitate him and keep on searching for

God every day, for being close to God brings us lots of blessings. God will give us comfort, strength, and courage to move forward each day and do the right things. Jacob evidently had a heated confrontation with his brother and had to be on the run. He also had an all-night struggle with a divine figure, trying to figure out what to do next. Was it an internal struggle with his own conscience? Or did he really have a wrestling match with God over his future? The Bible never made it clear for us on why Jacob had hand-to-hand combat with a divine figure. But the fact that he was able to see God face-to-face is an experience we all wish to have. Jacob certainly felt reassured and comforted after his two encounters with the Lord.

So far we have seen four meetings with the Lord as told in the Old Testament: The first couple (Adam and Eve) and the Lord; Cain and the Lord; Abraham and the Lord; and Jacob and the Lord. In the first three meetings, God seemed to appear for a specific, intended purpose. God showed up to take care of a particular task, and the subject did not have to call on God to come. God came to carry out an official task and let the witnesses soak in his presence. The divine presence compelled them to embrace the truth and do the right thing. If God had not appeared and confronted the first couple on their bad intention, we can only imagine how infectious it might have spread to the whole of creation. That divine encounter helped the first couple to see that it does not pay to disobey God's command. Likewise, God appeared to make Cain face up to his bad act and hopefully help him turn his life around. God's presence also helped Abraham realize that his love for God and his son was worth more than any sacrificial offering. God desires love and not some ritual. Abraham finally came to his senses and cancelled the sacrifice of his son. He proved his love for God by showing his love and care for his son. In these three cases, we have seen how God's presence could make a big difference to the people involved. God helped them see right from wrong and come to the right decisions when needed.

But God's presence can do much more for a person. Jacob realized how important it was to be close to God and kept on searching for God during his run from his brother, Esau. He thought about God throughout the day and asked God to help him avoid all the danger. He also came to God to ask for food, guidance, strength, and courage to keep moving forward. However, connecting to God during the day was not enough for him. Jacob wanted to stay in touch with God even at night and in his dreams. While he was asleep, he dreamt of a ladder extending from Earth to Heaven. We all know who lives in Heaven: God! In his lonely and scary night, he did not ask another human being to protect and help him. He ran to God for protection and tried to get connected to God in his dream. Most of us might think about God during the day but usually not while being asleep. By limiting our communication with God only to the day, we cut ourselves away from God the other half of the time. That would be like having to hold our breath for twelve hours before we can take in a deep breath, since God is our breath and life. Over time, our lack of breath (or God's presence) would add up, and our relationship with God would suffer tremendously.

Jacob realized how valuable God was in his life and, hence, maximized his connecting time with God by dreaming about a ladder extending to Heaven. His search for God did not stop there. He actually had a physical encounter with God and proudly recounted it. That encounter lasted all night long and made a great impact on Jacob. It gave him confidence and helped him deal with the challenges ahead of him. Jacob survived his brother's deadly hunt and became the leader of God's people because he relied on God's help and looked for God unceasingly.

Jacob eventually settled down and had his own family. One of his sons—Joseph—had to endure lots of mean treatments from his brothers and other life challenges. But he did not let those turn him into a cynical, bitter person or make him angry at God and run away from God. As he was sold and exiled to the foreign land and had to face tremendous hardship along the way, Joseph did not forget about God. Rather, he stayed close to God and continued to be connected to God throughout his life. He even tried to understand God's messages to the people through their dreams. He was blessed with that gift and later became an excellent dream interpreter. He was able to interpret dreams for a special client—the Egyptian king Pharaoh—and helped the king save his entire country from starvation for one drought season by storing away enough grains from previous harvests. Amidst all the praises and accolades from the king and the public, Joseph replied, "It is not I, but God who gives you eminent the right answer" (Genesis 41:16). King Pharaoh saw how valuable Joseph was to him and his kingdom. The king and all his subjects came to Joseph for counsel and guidance. That is one of many benefits of being in the presence of God: God gives us wisdom and the ability to see the future, like God's prophets. Joseph apparently was blessed with that ability, and he used it to help the king. But the king and his kingdom were not the only ones who benefited from Joseph's close relationship with God. His own family came to Egypt to find some food assistance, and Joseph was able to generously share God's blessings with them and save them from starvation.

Being close to God helped turn Joseph into a generous and merciful person. The Lord helped heal all his past hurt and dissipate the anger he had toward his brothers. He forgave them and extended his hands to assist them. If we do not remain in God's presence, we would not have any mercy toward our neighbors and reach out to help them in a time of need. God's presence challenges us to forgive and calls us to be like our God. Without being in God's presence, Jacob would have acted like a typical human being and carried out vengeful acts once he became powerful. Jacob eventually became the second most powerful person in Egypt, right behind King Pharaoh, but he did not use his newly found power to get back at people who had hurt him before. Rather, he reached out to his foes, forgave them, and helped them in times of need. Being close to God helped change Jacob and made him a better person. That is why he searched for God not only during the day but also in his dreams.

If there was someone in the Old Testament who could show us how to search for God and be close to God in our daily struggle, it would be Moses. He was a Hebrew kid who was abandoned by the riverbank and was found and adopted by Pharaoh's daughter. He grew up in Egypt and witnessed the mistreatment and killing of his own countrymen by the Egyptians. He was forced to defend a Hebrew and ended up killing an Egyptian. King Pharaoh heard about this and tried to capture him and put him to death. Moses had to go into hiding and continued to see terrible injustices being done toward his fellow Hebrews. Naturally, he called on God for help and kept on searching for God day and night for protection and guidance. One day, "There an angel of the Lord appeared to him in fire flaming out of a bush. As he looked on, he was surprised to see that the bush, though on fire, was not consumed. So, Moses decided, 'I must go over to look at this remarkable sight, and see why the bush is not burned'" (Exodus 3:2–3). Moses surely wanted to be around God and never stopped searching for God throughout the day. He knew that there were lots of wonderful benefits to having God in his life. He realized that the only one who could help him and free the people of God from the Egyptian slavery system was the Lord. That is why he searched high and low, even in the tree bushes, for the divine help and the best plan of escape from Egypt.

As Moses approached the burning bush to check it out, "God called out to him from the bush, 'Moses! Moses!' He answered, 'Here I am'" (Exodus 3:4). This was the first time in the Old Testament a person heard God call out his name and responded positively to it. We often do not see this personal exchange between God and a human being. But Moses was a special person, and God gave him an extraordinary treatment. This special relationship continued to grow as Moses kept searching for ways to be near God. Yet "Moses hid his face, for he was afraid to look at God" (Exodus 3:6). That is how most people would react in the presence of the almighty God. After his shy encounter with the Lord, Moses was assigned the task of rescuing the people of God from Egypt. One of the miracles God did for Moses and the people of God was to lead them out of Egypt. The Lord said to Moses, "Tell the Israelites to go forward. And you, lift up your staff and with hand outstretched over the sea, split the sea in two so that the Israelites may pass through it on dry land. But, I will make the Egyptians so obstinate that they will go in after them. … The Egyptians shall know that I am the Lord, when I receive glory through Pharaoh and his chariots and charioteers" (Exodus 14:15–18).

God was surely present with Moses and the people of God throughout this journey. Here is how they found God: "The angel of God, who had been leading Israel's camp, now moved and went around behind them. The column of cloud also, leaving the front, took up its place behind them, so that it came between the camp of the Egyptians and that of Israel" (Exodus 14:19–20). Only by the hand of God could the Israelites escape from the Egyptian army and truly experience the power of God. They recognized the power of God: "[W]hen Israel saw the Egyptians lying dead on the seashore and beheld the great power that the Lord had shown against the Egyptians, they feared the Lord and believed in him and in his servant Moses" (Exodus 14:30).

The Lord continued to reveal God's presence to Moses and the people of God through miracles in the desert, such as blessing them with quail and manna for food and producing water for them from the rock. The Lord also told Moses, "I am coming to you in a dense cloud, so that when the people hear me speaking with you, they may always have faith in you also" (Exodus 19:9). Besides revealing his presence by performing miracles for the people of God, God also appeared to them in a dense cloud and fire, as described in the following passage: "Whenever the cloud rose from the Dwelling, the Israelites would set out on their journey. But, if the cloud did not lift, they would not go forward; only when it lifted did they go forward. In the daytime the cloud of the Lord was seen over the Dwelling; whereas at night fire was seen in the cloud by the whole house of Israel in all the stages of their journey" (Exodus 40:36–38). The people of God must have felt safe and well-protected as they surrounded themselves with the presence of God. It did not matter day or night: God was always with them because they made sure they stayed close to God, the source of life.

The people of God did not just need God on their long journey. They also called on God to help them pick a new king. The Lord answered and said to Samuel, "How long will you grieve for Saul, whom I have rejected as king of Israel? Fill your horn with oil, and be on your way. I am sending you to Jesse of Bethlehem, for I have chosen my King from among his sons" (1 Samuel 16:1). Prophet Samuel was sent to do an important job for the people of God as he tried to choose the right person to be their king. He picked David to be the replacement for King Saul. That proved to be the correct choice, as David stood up to Goliath, the Philistine, and protected the people of God. He later proved to be the best king for the Israelites. If Prophet Samuel and the people of God had not stayed close to God, they would not have picked the right person to be their king, and the history of God's people would not have been the same. This is a very important lesson for us, as we have to make lots of decisions every day and throughout our lives. We must search for God at those moments and stay close to God if we want to make the right decisions or choices. King David and his son, King Solomon, would realize later how important it was for them to stay connected to God as they became the best leaders for the people of God.

For the people of God, the Ark of the Covenant represented the presence of God in their midst, and it brought them comfort and reassurance. They looked up to it for guidance and blessings. It was a great honor to be near the Ark of the Covenant, as described this way: "The Ark of the Lord remained in the house of Obededom the Gittite for three months, and the Lord blessed Obededom and his whole house. When it was reported to King David that the Lord has blessed the family of Obededom and all that belonged to him. David went to bring up the ark of God from the house of Obededom into the city of David amid festivities" (2 Samuel 6:11-12). Like the people of God, King David came to the Lord for guidance, protection, comfort, support, and most importantly, blessings. He wanted to stay close to the Lord to find blessings for him and his family. He would soon find out that the Lord would bring him much more, including a humble and contrite attitude to admit his wrongdoing.

The Bible reports, "The Lord sent Nathan to David, and when he came to him, he said: 'Judge this case for me! In a certain town there were two men, one rich and one poor. ... The rich man received a visitor ... and took the poor man's ewe lamb and made a meal of it for his visitor. ...' David grew very angry with that man and said to Nathan: 'As the Lord lives, the man who has done this merits death! He shall restore the ewe lamb four-fold because he has done this and has had no pity.' Then Nathan said to David: 'You are the man!'" (2 Samuel 12:1–7). God often used prophets like Nathan to communicate to the people of God and bring them judgments as well as blessings. Prophet Nathan came to David to point out his sin of adultery and murder and deliver to him God's punishment. The child who was born from this adulterous affair was condemned to die. David "besought God for the child. He kept fast, retiring for the night to lie on the ground clothed in sackcloth" (2 Samuel 12:16). But the Lord still carried out his punishment, and the child ended up dead. As we can see, David searched for God to ask for help, not for him but for an innocent child. We often think that we look for God in our daily life simply for our own needs. We completely forget that we can ask God to help others as well. The story of David above reminds us to look for God on behalf of others also.

If there is someone in the Old Testament who knew how to find God and came to God often, it would be David. He searched for God in the Ark of the Covenant, the prophets, and anywhere he thought God could be found around him. Sometimes, it was in the open field, and other times, it was in a closed shelter. He came to God for many things and consulted with God often. He asked God to help him in times of need and forgive him when he faltered. He was very proud of his close relationship with God and had an easy time coming to God among some prominent Old Testament figures like Abraham and Moses. Even when he offended God and committed grievous sins like adultery and murder, he was able to come to God and face the consequences of his actions without delay. David also wrote many psalms to express his feelings and relationships with the Lord. Among 150 psalms in the Bible, seventy-three psalms are attributed to David. Here is a sample of his writing: "O Lord, my rock, my fortress, my deliverer, my God, my rock of refuge! My shield, the horn of my salvation, my stronghold, my refuge, my savior, from violence you keep me safe. 'Praised be the Lord,' I exclaim, and I am safe from my enemies. ... In my distress I called upon the Lord and cried out to my God; from his temple he heard my voice, and my cry reached his ear" (2 Samuel 22:2–7).

David must have seen the importance of staying close to God and encouraged future generations to search for God in their daily lives. He helped us see the blessings of having God in our lives. By having God in his life, David had nothing to fear or worry about. He knew that God would defend and guide him throughout his life. Because of this life-fulfillment secret, he was able to maintain a prosperous and peaceful kingdom for the longest time in the history of the Israelites. He passed on this secret to his son King Solomon who tried to carry on his father's legacy during his reign. Here is David's instruction to his son Solomon: "I am going the way of all mankind. Take courage and be a man. Keep the mandate of the Lord, your God, following his ways and observing his statutes, commands, ordinances, and decrees as they are written in the law of Moses, that you may succeed in whatever you do, wherever you turn, and the Lord may fulfill the promise he made on my behalf when he said, 'If your sons so conduct themselves that they remain faithful to me with their whole heart and with their whole soul, you shall always have someone of your line on the throne of Israel'" (1 King 2:1–4). David counseled his son Solomon to search for God and follow the way of the Lord if he wanted the divine to protect and bless him.

Solomon realized how valuable his father's advice was and remained close to the Lord. He loved the Lord and obeyed all the commands and statutes of the Lord. He searched for ways to be with the Lord every chance he could and stayed attentive to the Lord's messages communicated to him daily. We learned that:

[I]n Gebeon the Lord appeared to Solomon in a dream at night. God said, "Ask for something of me and I will give it to you." Solomon answered: "You have shown great favor to your servant, your father David, because he behaved faithfully toward you, with justice and an upright heart; and you have continued this great favor toward him, even today seating a son of his on his throne. O Lord, my God, you have made me, your servant, King to succeed my father David; but I am a mere youth, not knowing at all how to act. ... Give your servant, therefore, an understanding heart to judge your people and to distinguish right from wrong." ... So, God said to him, "Because you have asked for this—not for a long life for yourself, nor for riches, nor for the life of your enemies, but for understanding so that you may know what is right[,] I do as you requested. I give you a heart so wise and understanding that there has never been anyone like you up to now, and after you there will be no one equal to you. In addition, I give you what you have not asked for, such riches and glory that among kings there is not your like. And if you follow me[,] keeping my statutes and commandments, as your father David did, I will give you a long life." When Solomon awoke from his dream, he went to Jerusalem, stood before the ark of the covenant of the Lord, offered holocausts and peace offerings, and gave a banquet for all his servants. (1 Kings 3:5–15)

Like some ancient figures, King Solomon first met the Lord in his dream and received certain instructions on what the Lord wanted him to do. He was asked to keep the Commandments and follow the way of the Lord if he wanted the Lord to guide and bless him. The Lord promised to grant him many blessings, and one of them was the gift of wisdom and right judgment. It took King Solomon many years of his governance before he realized how valuable that gift was, as he had to preside over many disputes in his kingdom. His wisdom and good judgment spread throughout the region, so much that the kings and queens of the neighboring countries came to visit him and seek counsel. After his first encounter with the Lord in a dream, King Solomon continued to search for the Lord around him every day. To help him meet the Lord in a formal setting and on a regular basis, King Solomon decided to build the Temple for the Ark of the Lord and worship it. Like the people of God and many of his ancestors, King Solomon found the Temple to be the best place to meet the Lord.

A few of them, like Abraham and Moses, were able to see the Lord even in nature and other informal settings. These two revered figures in the Jewish tradition often had an intimate encounter with the Lord on a high mountain. Abraham made a sacrificial offering to the Lord on the mountain, while Moses received the Ten Commandments. However, generally, it was not easy for the people of God to meet the Lord. They usually had to rely on the prophets or some holy figures to receive God's messages for them. They did not dare speak directly to the Lord. Even when they had a divine encounter, it was often with an angel of the Lord or some divine messenger. God remained a mystery and hidden from the people of God. Yet they could feel the divine presence and blessings or punishment realistically in their daily life. They were also encouraged to follow the way of the Lord and come to the Lord for help.

After the peaceful and prosperous time under the reign of Kings David and Solomon, the Israelites were conquered and driven into exile and slavery. They were subject to mistreatments and cruel punishments. Their lives seemed hopeless and faced a dead end. Tobit tried to help his fellow Israelites and bury his dead neighbors. But he was so overwhelmed by his life burdens and personal problems (namely, his blindness) that he broke down in tears. Here is how he described his state of mind at that moment: "Grief-stricken in spirit, I groaned and wept aloud. Then with sobs I began to pray: 'You are righteous, O Lord, and all your deeds are just; all your ways are mercy and truth; you are the judge of the world. And now, O Lord, may you be mindful of me, and look with favor upon me. Punish me not for my sins, nor for my inadvertent offenses, nor for those of my fathers. … It is better for me to die than to live, because I have heard insulting calumnies, and I am overwhelmed with grief. Lord, command me to be delivered from such anguish'" (Tobit 3:1–6). Tobit found himself overwhelmed with grief and life problems. He searched for the Lord for help and prayed that he would be free from all the miseries and perhaps from the current life altogether. He wanted to die and be done with his miserable life.

However, he was not the only person who felt miserable and wanted to be done with the present life. Raguel's daughter Sarah evidently was fed up by her misfortune and the insults of her mean neighbors after having seven husbands die on her. Her life was filled with sadness and misery. She did not know what to do, except ask God to end it for her. Like Tobit, Sarah desired death and expressed it in the following prayer: "And now[,] O Lord, to you I turn my face and raise my eyes. Bid me to depart from the earth, never again to hear such insults. … I have already lost seven husbands; why then should I live any longer? But, if it pleases you, Lord, not to slay me, look favorably upon me and have pity on me;

never again let me hear these insults" (Tobit 3:11–15). Sarah had reached the end of her limit and endurance. Like Tobit, she had lost her desire to live and her hope in humanity. People made fun of her misfortune and taunted her with messages like this: "You are the one who strangles your husbands! Look at you! You have already been married seven times, but you have had no joy with any one of your husbands. … Because your husbands are dead. Then, why not join them! May we never see a son or a daughter of yours" (Tobit 3:8–9).

It is horrible for Sarah to be treated like that. Both Sarah and Tobit could not find any sympathy from their neighbors. They felt alone and lost in an increasingly hostile and indifferent world. The only one they could count on to comfort them and listen to their concerns was God. Everyone else had either turned against them or showed them no sympathetic ears for their needs. They went in search of God to seek comfort, understanding, sympathy, help, hope, encouragement, and guidance. They came to God in prayer and poured out their sorrowful hearts and troubled spirits. They had nowhere to go to except God.

Another person who searched for God in times of trial was Job. He evidently lost his family and all his possessions as a test between the Devil and God. The Devil thought that if Job was pushed to an extreme test like that, even a faithful servant of God like him would curse and turn against God. However, Job never turned against God or did anything to destroy that relationship. Rather, "he cast himself prostrate upon the ground and said, 'Naked I came forth from my mother's womb, and naked shall I go back again. The Lord gave and the Lord has taken away; blessed be the name of the Lord!' In all this Job did not sin, nor did he say anything disrespectful of God" (Job 1:20–22). Job was an amazing servant of the Lord. His life was about obeying God's commands and following the way of the Lord. He came to God often to give thanks and praise. Suddenly, his life was turned upside down, and he lost everything, including his family. But he did not get angry at God or run away from God. He continued to look for God in his misfortune and trust that God would continue to guide him. He wanted to set a good example for future generations to stay close to God, the source of life even in tough times, because it would benefit them one way or another. He encouraged anyone who faced life challenges to be patient and trust that the Lord would come through in the end.

We often find ourselves running away from God in tough times. Or we might get angry at God when things do not turn our way. But if we relentlessly search for God like Job did, we will eventually find the right help for our problems. Sometimes, we might think God has abandoned us during challenging times. Or we might stop looking for God when times get tough. However, Job wants to remind us to stay close to God and find comfort in the Lord when we face death and tragedies in our lives, for that is how we could have strength and courage to make it through those dark nights of the soul. Otherwise, we would fall victim to depression and have no desire to live. By invoking God's presence in this difficult time, God will become a life raft for us to cling to and give us the courage to keep on living.

But we do not just come to God in times of personal tragedies. We also look for God during national calamity. Apparently, the Temple of Jerusalem was destroyed in 587 BC, and the whole country was exiled to Babylon. The people of God were humiliated and turned into slaves. One of them who witnessed the national humiliation expressed his shaky faith in the Lord and enduring hope in the suffering time: "Look, O Lord, upon her [Jerusalem] misery, for the enemy has triumphed! ... Look, O Lord, and see how worthless I have become! ... Look, O Lord, upon my distress: all within me is in ferment. ... Give heed to my groaning; there is no one to console me. All my enemies rejoice at my misfortune" (Lamentation 1:9, 11, 20–21). Like the rest of the country, this witness called on the Lord for help amidst distress and national tragedy.

The people of God rushed out to search for divine assistance and wondered if God still loved them, for the invaders turned their country to ruin and took them to Babylon as slaves. The people of God lost everything and had to face lots of difficulties and an uncertain future. They did not know whom to turn to in this dark time, except God. They came to God to find hope and reassurance as they tried to keep on living. They asked God to give them a hand on the new life journey and deliver them from the yoke of slavery. They also searched out for God to see what had caused them to suffer the misfortune. They wondered if their sins had made God punish and abandon them. They tried to figure out ways to restore their relationship with God.

Like personal tragedies, this national calamity was a great opportunity to wake up the people of God and their spiritual life. It helped renew their relationship with God and call them home to the true source of security and protection. Hence, one of the main reasons for the people of God to search for the Lord in the Old Testament was to find the right protector and good defender. They had to face many powerful neighbors with lots of resources and deadly weapons. They wanted a courageous king (like David) or a wise king (like Solomon) to defend them. They needed divine assistance to bring about a miracle that would destroy an entire powerful army, as Moses showed them at the Red Sea. They basically looked for God because they were weak and helpless. If they had been strong and powerful, perhaps they would not have needed to call on God for help. They might not have even come to God as their first resort in times of trouble. The idea of God might not have even interested them or entered their consciousness. But, in reality, God was truly needed throughout the Old Testament. The people of God realized that they were the underdog and needed God to help them stand up to other powerful neighboring countries. They also wanted God to help them build up a new world where justice and peace would be the motto for its daily living.

The desire for that new world was the main reason for the author of the book of Daniel to reach out to God and write this book. He was a young Jew who was taken early to Babylon and witnessed the bitter persecution of the Jews and the rise of the great nations of the ancient world against Yahweh, the Lord. He decided to write this book to strengthen and comfort the Jewish people in their ordeal. He believed that people of faith could resist worldly temptations and conquer adversity. Also, God would have control over daily events and bring about a new kingdom that would overthrow existing powers and last forever. Daniel went in search for God and hoped that the Lord would soon make his vision of a new kingdom come true. He described his encounter with the divine as follows: "I was still occupied with my prayer … when Gabriel, the one whom I had seen before in vision, came to me in rapid flight at the time of the evening sacrifice. He instructed me in these words: 'Daniel, I have now come to give you understanding. When you began your petition, an answer was given which I have come to announce, because you are beloved. Therefore, mark the answer and understand the vision'" (Daniel 9:20–23).

Daniel was blessed to meet a divine figure named Gabriel who let him see the vision of a new world as he relentlessly looked for God in prayer. He was praised for his desire to be close to the Lord and elated to have a glimpse of a new kingdom. The destruction of the Jerusalem Temple would be removed, and all the ruins before him would be replaced by new construction. That was the desire and expectation of the people of God as they endured the suffering and humiliation of being slaves. They hoped to put an end to the exploitation and evil treatments by their slave masters. They wanted the Lord to bring them a new kingdom where there would be no more suffering and injustice.

Because of our broken and imperfect world, God's people have needed to search for God and ask for divine assistance since the beginning of creation. They have wanted the Lord to bring them a new Temple of Jerusalem, along with a new world.

CHAPTER 3

HOW GOD WAS FOUND IN THE NEW TESTAMENT

The New Testament begins with the birth of Jesus, the son of God. But before that wonderful miracle came about, God revealed the divine plan to Mary through the appearance of the archangel Gabriel. Mary was startled to see an angel and to have a conversation with this divine figure. She never had an experience like that before. In fact, this marked a total change in the way God might reveal the presence of himself to the world, for in the Old Testament, God often revealed himself in an abstract way. People would report a divine presence but not give a detailed description of the messenger. They might say an angel of the Lord appeared to them, but there was no name or clear identification of the divine figure. The clearest description of the divine presence was a burning bush. Moses evidently witnessed this experience and heard the divine voice but was not able to give any more details about it. The Lord seemed so close to him but still far from his reach.

Mary was the first human being to see an angel with her own eyes and have a real dialogue with this divine figure. She felt blessed and humbled by the incredible experience. Yet she realized how extraordinary her encounter with this divine figure was. It gave her courage to accept her new assignment from the Lord and the strength to carry it out faithfully to the end. She understood the importance of these divine encounters in the lives of the faithful. That is why she has purportedly appeared to God's faithful people all over the world for years, for she wishes to keep God's people connected to God and help them find strength and inspiration from above on their journey of faith.

Mary's cousin's husband, Zechariah, was blessed with a similar experience and had an encounter with the same archangel Gabriel in the Temple. He met the divine figure in the familiar setting of a temple, while Mary did not. But unlike Mary, he did not put his total trust in the angel and the divine plan. Because of that, he was penalized and not able to speak until the birth of his son John the Baptist.

Another man in the New Testament who had a personal encounter with an angel was Joseph, Mary's husband and foster father of Jesus. His first encounter came right before he shared a common life with his new wife, Mary. He obediently listened to the angel and carried out God's plan by agreeing to be the foster father of Jesus. However, this was not the only encounter Joseph had with an angel in a dream. He had his second encounter when an angel told him to take the holy family out of the country and hide in Egypt, for the evil King Herod was looking for the newborn king Jesus and trying to kill him. Like his first encounter with an angel, Joseph obediently carried out the mission entrusted to him and took Mary and baby Jesus into hiding. Even the holy family had to endure lots of hardship and would need divine guidance and protection in difficult times. They would want to surround themselves with divine presence to get them assistance and safety throughout their lives.

Realizing the blessings of God in their lives, many people have been excited to welcome any sign of the divine presence in their lives, while others have never stopped searching for God all over the world. For example, the shepherds were startled and overjoyed when they saw the choir of angels singing in the sky at midnight in wide-open field. They were also elated upon seeing the divine baby Jesus as they arrived at the stable. Meanwhile, the magi had scanned the whole sky to search for any unusual thing and found a strange star. They tracked it down and met the divine baby Jesus in a manger with his parents. They felt honored and joyful when they found this special treasure and presented him with their gold, frankincense, and myrrh. We can see that both the shepherds and the magi searched for signs of God's presence in different ways. The shepherds did not go explicitly in search of some divine sign like the magi did. But in a subtle way, we can see that their hearts desired to have a glimpse of God and they could not wait to see God with their own eyes in the manger. On the other hand, the magi intensely looked for any extraordinary sign in the universe to help them see the mind of the Creator. Their efforts finally paid off as they found a strange star that appeared in the sky and eventually led them to the divine baby. In the end, both the shepherds and the magi were rewarded with the same thing, in spite of their different ways of searching for God in their lives. They were able to meet God in the human form, which was something that had never happened before in human history.

Besides these two groups of searchers, another person in the New Testament who could not wait to meet God, and later pointed out Jesus the Messiah to the whole world, was John the Baptist. Based on his experience of God, John recognized immediately who Jesus was and pointed him out: "Look, the Lamb of God, who takes away the sin of the world! This is the one I meant when I said, 'A man who comes after me has surpassed me because he was before me'" (John 1:29–30). John was indeed overjoyed when he saw Jesus. He could not believe God had finally revealed himself in human form. Throughout human history, God has appeared and communicated to the people of God in an angelic form or some hidden way. They have longed to see God with their own eyes right here on Earth. They have wanted to surround their daily lives with the presence of God. They have prayed for a messiah to help bring them closer to God and the kingdom of Heaven.

Prophets Simeon and Anna were both among the first people to witness that prayer come true as they saw baby Jesus presented in the Temple. Simeon joyfully praised God and said, "Sovereign Lord, as you have promised; you now dismiss your servant in peace. For my eyes have seen your salvation, which you have prepared in the sight of all people, a light for revelation to the Gentiles and for glory to your people Israel" (Luke 2:28–32). Both of these prophets were surprised and honored to see a divine figure like Jesus. That divine encounter made their dream come true and complete their lives on Earth. It changed their lives forever. They felt overjoyed and satisfied by this amazing encounter. The presence of God completed their dream, and they could die happily. Once they were in the presence of God, nothing else mattered. Likewise, we would feel the same way if we found ourselves near God. We would be secure, peaceful, and happy when we were around God. Every moment we were in the presence of God, we would have a taste of what Heaven would be like, and nothing in this life would matter to us anymore.

Another person in the New Testament who felt blessed to be in the presence of God and actually met Jesus, the Lamb of God, was John the Baptist. John was excited to see Jesus and told everyone to follow that divine figure. He did not view Jesus as his fierce competitor. Rather, he welcomed Jesus's presence and believed it to be a wonderful blessing for him and the people of God. His excitement spread out to his disciples, and many of them left him to follow Jesus. His meeting with a divine figure like Jesus gave him confidence in his mission and the courage to carry it out. He continued to call people to turn away from their sinful ways of life and come back to God. He confronted King Herod about his wrongful marriage and was imprisoned for preaching the truth. He ultimately laid down his life for helping people to see God and the truth.

Jesus, the son of God and the long-awaited Messiah, was the first divine figure that people saw with their own eyes in human history. They might have seen a prophet or had a divine apparition but had never met a divine figure in flesh and blood like Jesus. Only with time would people realize how special it would be to meet him. That was why the disciples did not completely know about Jesus and his mission until Easter. But one thing we know for sure is that people all wanted to meet Jesus and be in his divine presence. They looked for Jesus to find healing and forgiveness, to be freed of evil spirits and the power of darkness, to be fed and nourished, to hear his message of hope and comfort, and most importantly, to experience God's love.

People from various towns and villages kept going in search for him. Even non-Jewish people and sinners like Zacchaeus desperately tried to look for him. But Zacchaeus was short in stature and had to climb a tree to have a glimpse of Jesus. Meanwhile, a woman who was afflicted with a hemorrhage for years wished to touch his clothes to be healed. In fact, here is what one of the four gospels tells us about the relentless public search for Jesus: "When they found him on the other side of the lake, they asked him, 'Rabbi, when did you get here?' Jesus answered, 'I tell you the truth. You are looking for me, not because you saw miraculous signs, but because you ate the loaves and had your fill. Do not work for food that spoils, but for food that endures to eternal life, which the Son of Man will give you. On him God the Father has placed his seal of approval'" (John 6:25–27).

People flocked to Jesus, who represented the presence of God, and asked him to help solve their problems. They searched for him all day and anticipated all his moves in order to be in presence of God. That presence brought them peace, joy, hope, and much more. When they were around Jesus, wonderful things always happened, and nothing could scare them. They felt safe, secure, comforted, and hopeful while being in the presence of Jesus. All their daily worries and fear seemed to disappear. Jesus was able to give them a hand and lift them up from their life burden. He surrounded them with good news and miracles. They surely felt God's presence when they were with Jesus. They could see the divine presence in all his work. Below, we will attempt to categorize their divine experiences according to some of our familiar attributes. In other words, whenever we see these wonderful attributes, we know for sure God's footprints were there.

We all know God is *love*, as John the evangelist tells us in his gospel. But we have not seen an act of love from God besides the one on the Cross of Jesus. God's love for us on the Cross of Jesus is quite obvious. Without a doubt, that love reassures us of God's presence in our world, even in the darkest moments of our lives. However, we can find at least two more examples in the New Testament where God's presence is revealed through an act of *love*.

The first story that shows us God's presence through an act of *love* is Jesus's healing of a man with leprosy (Mark 1:40–45). This disease causes its victims to look disfigured and become contagious. People often shunned lepers, and society looked down them. They were treated like second-class citizens. They did not have many friends and could not hold down a job. Lepers usually became beggars and had to live alone. They had to suffer tremendously and live in destitution. It was in this context that Jesus reached out to a man with leprosy. He wanted to show this lonely, dejected man love and compassion and bring him back to the human family. That act of love and care must have surprised the leper. No one had dared to touch him and be kind to him like that before. But he did not only see Jesus in that encounter; he experienced the presence of God, who brought him love, joy, hope, and reasons to live. The presence of God gave him a boost of confidence and brought him the miracle of cleansing. He was free from leprosy and a life of shame and loneliness. He experienced God's presence by Jesus's simple act of love and compassion. We could do the same thing for someone by a simple act of love and care. We could help a person experience the presence of God by reaching out and sharing a kind and loving act.

A second story that reveals the presence of God through an act of *love* is Jesus's feeding of the 4,000 (Matthew 15:29–39). If healing and bandaging people shows them our care, feeding them conveys a similar message. In some cultures, making good food for a visitor is a perfect way to show one's hospitality. By taking care of people's basic needs, we express our love and care for them. But that is more than just a kind act; we might even help them see how God would look like through an act of love. Most of the 4,000 people might not have seen God before meeting Jesus. However, after seeing what Jesus did for them, they must have identified him as their God. He saw them getting hungry and came to their rescue. He fed 4,000 hungry mouths and helped them meet a caring God. Only God can take care of that big of a number of people without much preparation and resources. No one had ever been kind to them like that before. This was the first time they had experienced an act of love and compassion.

The only one who loved and cared for them like that was God. Jesus did more than just a miracle; he showed them the face of God and let them experience God's love and compassion. Therefore, whenever we do an act of love and reach out to the neglected or the needy, we imitate Jesus and show the world the face of God. The world will be able to meet God and experience God through an act of love. The more we want the world to experience God, the more acts of love we need to do every day. Indeed, when God is with us, great and wonderful things will happen, as we see with the examples above about the leper and the hungry crowd.

Besides an act of love, we can help the world find God through an act of *mercy*. When we act mercifully to someone, we help that person meet God, for our world often judges and condemns people. It is not afraid to be mean and treat people badly. After all, it is a dog-eat-dog world. But God does not want his people to eat and treat one another like the world does. God needs his people to behave differently and become like their God instead of the world, for their God is full of mercy. By showing acts of mercy, Jesus wants to reveal that part of God to the world. Jesus wants us to know that our God is merciful and calls us to imitate that quality of God.

The first example of *mercy* Jesus wanted to show us was about a woman who was caught in an act of adultery (John 8:1–11). Apparently, the teachers of the law and the Pharisees wanted to trick Jesus and put him between a rock and a hard place, between the law of Moses and the law of God. The law of Moses would condemn an adulterer to be stoned to death, as the teachers of the law and the Pharisees tried to tell Jesus. However, the law of God would tell them, "Love God with all your heart and soul, and love your neighbor as yourself." What they did not realize was the fact that Jesus represented their God, who is full of mercy and forgiving. He wanted them to meet their God by experiencing the divine quality of mercy.

He posed them this premise: "If any one of you is without sin, let him be the first to throw a stone at her." By saying that, Jesus wanted them to reexamine their own sinful lives and give thanks to God for the divine mercy he gave them every day. Hopefully, that way, they might learn to share the same mercy and show God's presence to people around them. Then Jesus turned to the woman and asked her, "Woman, where are they? Has no one condemned you?" She said, "No one, sir." Jesus declared, "Neither do I condemn you. Go now and leave your life of sin." The woman certainly experienced God's mercy and met God that day. She found a new life with God. Perhaps the teachers of the law and the Pharisees did the same. We all wish to be blessed with the same experience. Thankfully, the same experience can be repeated in our time. Whenever we act mercifully, we repeat what Jesus did and show the world God's mercy and presence.

Another example Jesus did to show God's *mercy* and presence to our world was his meeting with Zacchaeus, the tax collector (Luke 19:1–10). Zacchaeus made his living by being a tax collector and engaging in that sinful way of life. His occupation led him to cheat and blackmail people on taxes to benefit himself personally. He accumulated his massive wealth and, along with it, public resentment. He heard about Jesus and his message of God's mercy. He decided to find Jesus and check it out for himself. He did not mind climbing a sycamore-fig tree to have a glimpse of Jesus, who was a divine figure according to the public. But he got more than he intended. Jesus saw him and called, "Zacchaeus, come down immediately! I must stay at your house today." Why did Jesus want to stay at Zacchaeus's home? Did he want Zacchaeus to give him free room and board because of his wealth? Jesus wanted to visit Zacchaeus because he felt his host deserved God's mercy and a new life.

Zacchaeus was sincere in his search for God's mercy and a personal conversion. Jesus saw his heart and believed in him. The public did not want Jesus to let Zacchaeus experience God's mercy and accused him of embracing sinners. But the truth is that sinners need God's mercy more than anyone else. Zacchaeus was so grateful for God's mercy and his meeting with a divine figure like Jesus. He confessed, "Look, Lord! Here and now I give half of my possessions to the poor, and if I have cheated anybody out of anything, I will pay back four times the amount." Jesus responded, "Today, salvation has come to this house." Jesus indeed confirmed that God was present at Zacchaeus's home that day, and the host did experience God's mercy. Therefore, whenever we reach out and perform an act of mercy, we relive what Jesus did and let the person experience God's presence in our world. This experience is worth more than any worldly possessions.

If the two attributes *love* and *mercy* are often associated with God, most people do not think about God when they talk about *peace*. Otherwise, they would not constantly cause wars and fighting like we see in our human history, for that would be like trying to push God out of the world after everything God did for the whole of creation. Because of their detachment from peace and God, most people often talk about peace in terms of the absence of wars and conflicts, while still ignoring God completely. But the truth is that our world cannot experience peace without embracing God. True peace only comes from God, who will let our world experience the fruits of peace. To help us see that connection better, let us examine two examples in the New Testament.

The first example of *peace* is the story of Jesus calming the storm (Mark 4:35–41). Jesus and his disciples were in the boat at sea when a storm broke out. Strong winds tossed the boat around, and the towering waves crashed over the boat, while Jesus was asleep in the stern. The disciples were scared and called out to Jesus, "Teacher, don't you care if we drown?" Jesus got up, rebuked the wind, and said to the waves, "Quiet! Be still!" Then the wind died down, and it was completely calm. There was nothing the disciples desired more than a peaceful sea. As they crossed the sea of life, they ran into all sorts of storms of life. Those storms shook them up and scared their resolve about following Jesus. At those scary and doubtful moments, the disciples thought Jesus had abandoned them and did not care whether they would die or live. As they tried to find peace in their hearts, they had to call out to Jesus and ask God to put an end to the turmoil around them. Jesus answered their call and came to their rescue. He delivered them from the rough seas and restored peace to their lives.

As we can see, true peace can come only from God. God alone will bless us with peace. When God is present in our lives, we will have peace. Likewise, when peace is in our world, God must be there.

The second example of God's presence wherever there is *peace* can be seen when the risen Christ appeared to his fearful disciples (Luke 24:36–49). Right after their Lord Jesus was arrested, crucified, and buried, the disciples were in hiding and fearful for their lives. They locked the doors and barricaded their hiding place. They thought God had abandoned them, and their future was uncertain. While the disciples were in the state of confusion and anxiety, Jesus appeared in their midst and said to them, "Peace be with you." Jesus's presence without a doubt boosted their confidence and restored their trust in God, for they were lost and scared after his burial. But Jesus also brought them peace and a new life. After their encounter with the risen Christ, they were no longer fearful of anything, including the persecuting authority. They felt at peace and, at the same time, compelled to go out and tell the whole world the fantastic news about the risen Christ. They were completely changed from a group of scared disciples to an army of brave witnesses for their master. That is what the presence of the risen Christ did to them. Imagine if we had his presence with us every day; we would be able to change and do lots of great things as well. But before the disciples could go through that miraculous transformation, they had to experience peace from the risen Christ. His presence calmed them down and brought them peace. Indeed, peace and the presence of God go hand in hand. Wherever we find peace, there we will experience the presence of God also.

We have seen how God has revealed himself through acts of *peace*, *mercy*, and *love*. Next, we will show how an act of *joy* has been used in the Gospels to let us know about the presence of God in our world. The first example that God has shown his presence through a *joyful* occasion is the Christmas story (Luke 2:1–20). In this story we learn how God entered our world and touched many lives with the joyous news of Christmas. The first people who were touched by that wonderful news were Elizabeth and her baby in the womb, John the Baptist. When Mary, who was pregnant with Jesus, came to visit Elizabeth's family, the joyous news of Jesus's birth caused baby John jump in his mother's womb. Baby John apparently sensed the presence of the son of God and rejoiced at that blessed encounter. That joyous meeting was a great encounter between baby John and God. A similar meeting like this happened between God's representative and Mary, as the angel Gabriel told her about the joyous news of her conception of baby Jesus. That joyous news continued to reach the shepherds in the field and the magi in the east. Like the last reception of the joyous news of baby Jesus by baby John, the shepherds and the magi welcomed it with great excitement and could not wait to meet the divine figure. They felt it was a distinguished honor to meet baby Jesus. Wherever people heard about the joyous news of Christmas, they would surely have met the divine figure in the form of baby Jesus. Likewise, wherever we can find joy, God will surely be found. Our job is to create lots of joyful occasions so that we can meet God easily every day.

Another Gospel story to help us see the connection between a *joyous* occasion and the divine presence is the Easter story (Matthew 28:1–10). Jesus was taken down from the Cross and buried in the tomb before a huge stone was rolled against the entrance. All of his followers thought it was the end of their leader and the Christian movement. Everyone left the tomb full of sorrow and disappointment. Some thought about going back to their old way of life while others tried to avoid the authority and the same fate of their master. Mary Magdalene and a few women were the only ones who dared to go out to the tomb and check on their master. Upon their visit, "[T]here was a violent earthquake, for an angel of the Lord came down from Heaven and, going to the tomb, rolled back the stone and sat on it." The angel then said to the women, "Do not be afraid, for I know that you are looking for Jesus, who was crucified. He is not here; he has risen, just as he said. Come and see the place where he lay." So the women hurried away from the tomb, afraid yet filled with joy. They had not expected this joyful news when they went out to visit Jesus's tomb. Like all the joyful meetings in the New Testament, they met an angel of the Lord and, later, the risen Lord himself. Evidently, wherever a divine figure appears, we can find joy and great wonders. Similarly, if we want to meet God, we just need to create a joyful occasion as one of the best ways to invite God to enter our world.

If *joy*, *peace*, *mercy*, and *love* are some of the easiest ways to bring us closer to God, *hope* is another opportunity to assure us a divine encounter. When we hope for something, we anticipate and look forward to its coming. When we hope to meet God, we go in search for all the available opportunities and do our best to prepare for that encounter. If we have a hopeful outlook, we will have an easier time of meeting God. We also need to be open to various ways that God might reveal himself in our world in spite of our daily challenges. When we are hopeful, we will allow God to enter our lives and be ready to welcome God at any time. We will also believe that God will come to our rescue in the end. In fact, there are two examples in the Gospels to help us see why God usually shows up wherever there is *hope*.

The first example about *hope* is the story of Jesus appearing to Mary Magdalene (John 20:10–18). Although she was scared and confused about Jesus's death and mission, like the rest of the disciples, she never lost hope in her master. She continued to hold on to a slim hope that God had a plan for her Lord Jesus and would not let him get rotten in the tomb. She went out to the tomb to check on him as John's Gospel reported: "Mary stood outside of the tomb crying. As she wept, she bent over to look into the tomb and saw two angels in white, seated where Jesus's body had been, one at the head and the other at the foot. ... She turned around and saw Jesus standing there. ... Jesus said to her, 'Mary.' She turned toward him and cried out in Aramaic, 'Rabboni!'—which means Teacher." Her hopeful attitude about Jesus was rewarded handsomely, as she was allowed to meet the two angels and the Lord himself. That divine encounter was personal and emotional, as Jesus called her by name. But it was quite common that our divine encounters would be a personal experience. We all would have to meet God on our own instead of having that special experience through someone else. In response to her personal meeting with the risen Christ, Mary Magdalene called him "Teacher." For her, Jesus was not just the Lord but also a mentor, teacher, and friend. We would have a similar experience like Mary Magdalene did if we could maintain a hopeful attitude and try to bring hope to the world in everything we do.

Another example of *hope* that we can find in the Gospels is the story of the two disciples on the road to Emmaus (Luke 24:13–35). After the death of Jesus, some of his disciples decided to return to their old way of life. But they still hoped that something wonderful would come out of the whole tragedy with the suffering and death of Jesus. Here is their response to the inquiring visitor on the road to Emmaus: "Are you the only visitor to Jerusalem who does not know of the things that have taken place there in these days? ... The things that happened to Jesus the Nazarene, who was a prophet mighty in deed and word before God and all the people, how our chief priests and rulers both handed him over to a sentence of death and crucified him. But we were hoping that he would be the one to redeem Israel; and besides all this, it is now the third day since this took place." Clearly, these two disciples were sad and confused about the whole passion of their master. Yet they still held on to a slight hope that Jesus would be the long-awaited Messiah who would bring them salvation and other wonderful blessings. Their hopeful attitude amidst a depressing time allowed God to open their hearts to new wonders and let them have a divine experience. That brief experience gave them courage and excitement to commit themselves to carry on Jesus's mission and witness to his Easter miracle. Similarly, if we are filled with spirit of hope, we will surely have a divine encounter and be able to overcome any life challenge. For we will allow God to guide us and walk with us through some of the most difficult parts of our lives. The spirit of hope will infuse us with the incredible strength and resilience that can only be found in God to overcome any life challenge.

Like the five other attributes of *love*, *mercy*, *peace*, *joy*, and *hope* mentioned above, *generosity* is another indicator that will guarantee us the divine presence and bring us close to God. Generous people act and think like God, without discriminating the good against the bad in this life. They have the heart of God, which allows them to share their lives with others unconditionally. Throughout the Bible, we learn how God expresses this wonderful virtue with his people and comes to their rescue in times of need. Without this extraordinary virtue, God would behave like all humans and allow selfishness to control all aspects of the divine life. Jesus certainly is rooted in this virtue of generosity, as he had allowed it to guide his entire ministry. His generous nature moved him to reach out to the outcasts and the lowly, and do things beyond the normal routines and the Jewish community. His generosity brought the presence of God and all sorts of miracles to the people of God during his ministry. Likewise, we can do the same thing if we act and think generously every day. Here are a couple of examples in the Gospels to help us see the connection between generous living and the presence of God a little better.

The first example of *generosity* is the story of the wedding in Cana (John 2:1–11). The wedding couple apparently invited Jesus, among other guests, to their reception. Their generous spirit surely touched the Lord and his mother, who later encouraged him to get involved and help the couple when they ran out of wine. If they had not thought generously and had acted like some wedding couples who trim down their guest list, Jesus and his mother might not have been present, and they would not have been able to experience a miracle in their time of need. Our high-tech society teaches us to be efficient and trim everything down to the minimum. Our cultural time tells us to look inward and care only for ourselves. We view immigrants and anyone who does not look or act like us to be a threat to our livelihood and comfort zone. That pushes us to look more inward and become less generous in our thoughts and actions. We get angry easily and blame everything wrong in our lives on the "outside" threats like the immigrants. We selfishly keep everything for ourselves and do not want to share anything with others. God certainly cannot do any wonders for our world with that kind of attitude. Most of the miracles happened in the Bible when people opened their hearts to God and learned to share their meager resources with others. God then was able to use those things and create wonderful miracles for the world. In the story of the wedding in Cana, we see how Jesus was able to show God's presence and perform an awesome miracle for the couple and their guests because of their generous invitation of him and his mother to the event. If they had been stingy and kept Jesus off of their guest list, they would not have experienced that great miracle and found God's presence in a tough time. Also, if Jesus had not acted generously and tried to help the couple, we would not have seen any miracle and found God's presence at this wedding reception. When we think and act generously toward God and people around us, we will surely meet God and experience all kinds of miracles.

Another example to help us see the connection between the *generous* spirit and the presence of God is the story of the Syrophoenician woman (Mark 7:24–30). A Greek woman came to Jesus and asked him to help her little daughter, who was possessed by an evil spirit. At first, Jesus refused to reach out and help this non-Jewish woman. Then her faith in him moved him to act generously and extend her a helping hand. He drove the demon out of her little daughter and helped this family find God's presence in their lives again. If Jesus had decided to keep God's blessings to the Jews only, that miracle would never have happened and the Greek family would not have experienced God's presence. Evil and darkness would have ruled over the life of the little girl. Her mother and family would have continued to live in sadness and worry. Jesus's generous spirit helped bring God's presence to the little girl and her family. When we share that same spirit in our daily life, we give God more opportunities to do miracles and reveal God's presence to us. On the contrary, if we behave selfishly and refuse to help out others, we will never find God around us or experience any miracle in our daily life. A generous spirit would compel us to invite God into our lives and give God more opportunities to perform miracles in our world.

Finally, we have seen how *love, mercy, peace, joy, hope,* and *generosity* might help us experience God's presence easily in our lives. *Faithfulness* is another wonderful virtue to bring God closer to us. Throughout the Bible, we see how God demanded his people to be faithful and not to worship other idols. People who have been faithful to God have a better chance of meeting God and experiencing miracles in their lives. Some of the faithful people in the Bible are Abraham, Moses, Elijah, Job, Jacob, David, Mary, Joseph, Paul, and so on. These people had a special relationship with God and were able to have lots of divine encounters throughout their lives. Some of them received special tasks at those encounters, while others simply had a glimpse of God and a taste of a life in Heaven. Everyone who met God had a dramatic life transformation and wanted to see God again. We could replicate those encounters and invite God to perform more miracles in our lives by being a faithful servant of God. In fact, Jesus always demanded people to have faith if they wanted him to perform a miracle. *Faith* is a pair of eyeglasses that we need to put on if we want to see God and experience a miracle.

One example about *faith* and divine encounter in the Gospels is the healing of the woman with a hemorrhage (Mark 5:21–43). This poor woman had suffered a horrible bleeding problem for over twelve years. She had sought help from many medical doctors, but her problem had only grown worse. She heard about Jesus and decided to seek him out. Unfortunately, the crowd was too big for her to get in front of him to present her problem. Her faith in

Jesus compelled her to touch his clothes and that would be enough to bring her healing. Right after that, her bleeding stopped, and she was completely cured. Her faith in the Lord encouraged her to seek him out and led her to experience a spectacular miracle. We can meet God and experience the same thing every day if we live faithfully under God's Commandments. God will reveal his presence to us in various ways. God will pour down his blessings and miracles on us as the reward for our faithfulness. Our faithfulness to God also calls us to be faithful to our spouses, families, friends, vocations, church, country, and so on. *Faithful* people can see God everywhere and recognize miracles around them every day.

Another example in the Gospels that can help us see the connection between *faith* and divine experience is the story of the healing of the centurion's servant (Luke 7:1–10). A centurion heard about Jesus's healing ability and went in search of him. He had a highly valued servant who fell ill and was about to die. He wanted Jesus to heal this servant but confessed that he did not deserve the Lord to come to his home. He humbly asked Jesus to grant his servant a healing word from afar, and that would be enough for him. His amazing faith in Jesus brought about another wonderful miracle and healing of his servant. Jesus praised the centurion: "I tell you, I have not found such great faith even in Israel." The centurion's faith brought Jesus to him and his home. When Jesus is around, wonderful things happen. In case of the centurion, his servant was healed. If he had not shown his faith in Jesus, he would not have seen that great miracle. Similarly, when we show our faith in God, we invite God into our lives and homes. We will also create opportunities for God to do miracles in our world. Interestingly, our current world has not been faithful to God in everything it has done. Yet it has consistently expected God to perform nonstop miracles. It gets mad at God when it cannot get what it wants. If we want God to be near us and miracles to pop up all around us, we must learn to be faithful to God and others. This great virtue will give God more reasons to hang around us. It will also help us find miracles easily in good times and in bad.

CHAPTER 4

WHETHER GOD IS STILL NEEDED IN A HIGH-TECH AND COMFORTABLE SOCIETY, AND HOW GOD CAN BE FOUND IN MODERN TIMES

In the last two chapters, we have seen how people found God in the Old Testament and New Testament and why God was needed in their lives. In this chapter, we will examine how God may be found in modern times and whether God might be needed in our high-tech and comfortable society. We are surrounded by modern conveniences and daily routines. We constantly have to deal with high-tech solutions for every aspect of our lives. Our fast-paced and busy life makes it quite difficult for us to find God throughout our day. Our modern and secular world does not make it easy for us to recognize God in everything around us either. But true believers do not let those things keep them from meeting God daily, for God can do all sorts of miracles and bring them lots of blessings. If we stay close to God, we will always feel secure and at peace, in spite of our daily challenges. We will find hope, joy, and other blessings in our daily life.

We usually find God in typical worship places such as churches, temples, synagogues, mosques, and so on. But more and more people find God in nontraditional places these days. One of those new places for us to find God in modern-day society is nature. Indeed, God may exist in nature because God created it in the beginning. Some of the locations in nature for us to meet God could be a majestic mountain, a magnificent waterfall, or a mysterious jungle. Other locations might be a quiet sand dune, a soft-running creek, or an isolated piece of wooded land. If we live in the city, we might find God's presence in a park, a walking/biking trail, or a sports field. Because of our busy schedule and modern-day influence, some of us might not be religious and want to go to church every Sunday, but still believe in God. We might identify God's presence in nature and like to be around nature on Sunday instead of in a church or a temple.

The church might consider this viewpoint of God to be unacceptable and part of the "new age." Perhaps, this new-age phenomenon might not be orthodox and endorsed by the church. But it is the byproduct of the modern-day culture and secular society regarding faith and religion. Thankfully, people still believe in God and want to find God in their lives. The church simply needs to accept this new phenomenon and figure out how to work the new-age viewpoint of God into its traditional theology. Otherwise, the new-age believers might follow our secular and materialistic society and gradually become atheists.

The new-age believers or people who search for God in nature can trace their belief back to the first story of the Bible. In the book of Genesis, we were told how God could be found in nature, for God created the whole universe, including nature and everything in it. God continued to express his presence throughout creation. The first couple, Adam and Eve, found God and communicated with God in a nature setting. God even tested them in the outdoor by forbidding them to eat from a certain tree. Unfortunately, they failed the test and were punished by being exiled into an unknown future. But, they were not only the ones who found God in Nature. Noah and many well-known figures of the Old Testament like Abraham and Moses talked to God and had many divine experiences in an open field. We should not be surprised to see that many people of our time have decided to search for God in nature instead of the traditional way of being in churches, temples, and mosques. Most people of God in the biblical period did not run to the temples to look for God and worship until the First Temple was built. They all went out to God's beautiful creation and had a personal conversation with God. Therefore, we should not look down on anyone who might prefer to find God in nature instead of being in the building of a church, temple, or mosque.

We certainly can name some magnificent places in nature around the world where God can be found. Obviously, the best place of all is Yellowstone National Park. This breathtaking piece of land is filled with magnificent mountains, like Grand Tetons, and spectacular geysers, like Old Faithful. It also has lots of running streams, sheer cliffs, mysterious forests, and abundant wild creatures. Yellowstone National Park reminds people a lot of the Garden of Eden. In the Garden, the first couple got free access to God and felt peaceful and happy. They got everything they wanted, while God watched over them. In our time, the parks give us a sense of the divine presence and help us see the wonderful work God has done in creation. Most of us who have been through a park generally have fond memories of it and cannot wait to return to it. A park is usually serene and full of beautiful scenic views. If it does not put us back in the Garden of Eden, it at least makes us feel the presence of God. We often feel relaxed and peaceful in a park as we take a walk around it or hang around there with friends. We tend to forget our worries and challenges when we spend time in a park. Time seems to stand still, and we like to soak in everything nature might offer us in a park. Interestingly, that is how people who experience a divine encounter feel. They want that moment to last forever. We just need to ask the three apostles—Peter, James, and John—who were with Jesus on Mount Tabor and experienced his transfiguration, and we would see that they did not want that experience to end.

Some of us might not be able to take a trip to Yellowstone Nation Park or similar destinations. But we can still go hunting or fishing and commune with nature. If we have ever talked with hunters or fishermen about their upcoming trips to the wilderness or the lakes, we see how excited they feel. They look forward to spending time alone with nature or enjoying God's creation in the company of their loved ones and friends. Besides having some time for rest and relaxation, hunters or fishermen like to go back to the simple time of human existence and be freed of all the modern-day distractions. Some of them might enjoy these trips to clear their minds from daily worries and push the "refresh" button for their lives. Or they might look forward to some alone time to meet God and experience something extraordinary. They often feel rejuvenated and excited about reengaging with their lives after those trips. Like these hunters and fishermen, some of us go on retreats to meet God and perhaps have a personal conversion. We feel renewed after the spiritual trip to the mountain of God and find the strength to continue the mission God has entrusted to us on our faith journey.

Perhaps we cannot afford a hunting or fishing trip. But we might be able to take a walk in a park or ride a bike on a trail. In a serene and uplifting environment like that, we definitely feel much closer to God compared to sitting at home. We can also get in touch with our soul and spirit much more easily. Our hearts and mind can commune with nature and feel relieved from our daily challenges. When we face our daily routines and life challenges, sometimes we feel overwhelmed and anxious to be able to hear God talk to us. But in a park or on a trail, we can hear God's messages for us much more clearly. Our walk or bike ride helps clear our mind and pick out God's presence easily around us. When we feel relaxed or at peace, we can meet God easily. Once we have a divine encounter, many wonderful things can happen. We will have peace and joy in our hearts in spite of our life burdens. We will have extra strength to deal with our daily challenges and the wisdom to make right choices in this life. We will have the humility to ask for God's mercy and the courage to forgive our enemies.

However, nature is not the only setting in which many people of our time prefer to search for God and have a religious experience. A good number of people these days love to volunteer their time at God's Kitchen or get involved with a community project. They like to make a difference in the lives of others by reaching out and helping someone in need. They want to serve the poor and the hungry a bowl of soup at God's Kitchen. They love to build a home for a low-income family in the Habitat for Humanity program. They enjoy helping out with a community project like putting together a playground for kids. They like to get involved with a halfway house, abuse-and-neglect centers, or homeless shelters.

All those social justice projects help them recognize God's blessings in their lives and learn to reach out to people in need. Those projects also give them opportunities to meet the poor and the misfortunate and see God in those folks, for the Bible says that God created all humans in God's image. These encounters definitely train them to have the Lord's compassion for the poor and the misfortunate. Unfortunately, over time they will turn away from churches and temples and get more involved with God's Kitchen or community projects instead, for they feel that religious folks simply talk about loving one's neighbors, but in reality, sadly, they do not act on it.

They truly want to be people of action and do something to take care of the poor and the misfortunate. They see God's presence in the acts of mercy and kindness. They no longer view God in terms of concepts and theological ideas. They do not want to get tied into an institutional church or a set of human laws and regulations. They do not like to worship a god that is too far away from them. Their god must be closer to them and more personal. Like a doubting Thomas, they want to be able to touch and feel their God before they will believe. They need to examine and experience God personally and do not like to hear about it through others. God has to be real and personal for modern-day Christians. Otherwise, religion and faith do not matter to them at all. That remains true until God knocks on their doors through a personal conversion, or a tragedy or a difficult situation that forces them to meet God.

We sometimes wonder whether we could survive in the twenty-first century without divine assistance. On one hand, modern life is much more convenient and full of choices. Everything is much more readily available now compared to before. We have lots of resources at our disposal and a false sense of security. On the other hand, we have become much more individualistic and self-focused nowadays. Everything is simply about *me*. The idea of community is often associated with communism or socialism, which is most hated in the Western world. We also proudly assume that we can do anything on our own. But we have not yet figured out how to reduce our daily stress and life challenges. We obviously do not know how to achieve happiness either.

The only way we try to lessen our pains and deal with our life difficulties is alcohol and drugs. We take pills and other substances to give ourselves a false sense of reality and a temporary solution. We often find ourselves feeling anxious and overwhelmed by our daily challenges because we do not have enough resources and strength to deal with them. We eventually realize that the only one who can help us take care of our daily challenges and give us reasons to keep on living is God. The Lord can also bring us peace and true happiness. The Lord is the best source of nourishment for our soul and spirit. If our soul is not nurtured or our spirit is not strengthened, our body will slowly fall apart and die. The Lord plays an important role in our well-being. By staying close to the Lord, we ensure our well-being and survival. The Lord also brings us all kinds of miracles and blessings with his presence, as told in the Bible.

CHAPTER 5

HOW AN ORDINARY PERSON FINDS GOD THROUGHOUT THE WEEK

When I was in the seminary, a group of Buddhists held their weeklong retreat on our campus. Some of us came back to the seminary a bit early to get the tail end of this retreat. Part of it involved the ritual of pausing every fifteen minutes when we heard the gong sound. We were supposed to stop everything we were doing and pause for a minute to take a deep breath to recognize our presence and be thankful to the Creator for it.

At first, most of us seminarians found the whole idea of pausing every fifteen minutes a bit silly. We basically were frozen like a statue and stopped whatever we were doing at midstream to be a part of this ritual. We all had many things to do and were busy with our daily chores as we prepared for a new school year. This ritual would interrupt our nicely scheduled day and make us pause for a moment of consciousness. Besides, we were not Buddhists and not obliged to participate in this ritual with the retreatants. But as the owners of the retreat place, we did not want to be rude to our guests, and hence, we reluctantly participated in it.

After an hour and a few pauses, we did not mind going through with this ritual at all. Like a yoga exercise, it helped us to slow down in our busy lives and learn to appreciate every breath we took. People with ill health know how precious the gift of life is, and they are grateful for each breath. Anyway, we slowly began to realize how special this ritual was. It forced us to stop our busy schedule and acknowledge our existence by listening to our breath. In that process, we learn to appreciate everything we had, including our breath and our life. We also needed to give credit to the one who created us and continued to sustain us. Without God, we would not exist or be able to take in another breath.

I continued to think about that valuable ritual after all the Buddhist retreatants left our campus. They clearly left great impact on me with that spiritual exercise. I have begun to see how I have taken for granted my healthy life, as well as the one who created me. I need to be thankful for everything I have received each day and learn to appreciate my benefactors, including God, the biggest one of all. If I can keep myself close to God every moment of the day, I will certainly have everything I need. God might even let me experience a miracle now and then.

That is why I think it is crucial for us to search for God every day and everywhere we are allowed to do so. In this chapter, I have strategically mapped out a tentative schedule for our week to see how we can find God throughout our week. Hopefully, that will give us some ideas on how to find God's presence in our life and inspire us to do that more every day. God will protect us and guide us through all the windings of our life. God will also bring us true peace and happiness right here on Earth. God will let us experience miracles in challenging times. God is like the precious treasure hidden from our sight since creation, and we have to search for it and have it. Our life will be positively transformed if we have a hold of that precious treasure.

Monday: Finding God in a Family or a Home

"The Serenity Prayer" by Reinhold Niebuhr:

> God grant me the serenity to accept the things I cannot change; courage to change the things I can; and wisdom to know the difference. Living one day at a time, enjoying one moment at a time; accepting hardships as the pathway to peace; taking, as Jesus did, this sinful world as it is, not as I would have it; trusting that God will make all things right if I surrender to God's will; that I may be reasonably happy in this life and supremely happy with God forever in the next. Amen.

We might think finding God in a family is easy. But it is hard to do. Our family might have diverse opinions and beliefs. One person might want to do this, while another does that. A family member might hold a certain belief, while another holds a different one. The head of a household sure finds it difficult to have everyone sing from the same song sheet and create an atmosphere of sweet harmony. Additionally, our family can be a source of complaints and criticism. Our children might whine about all kinds of things, while our in-laws can be the thorn in our side with their criticism. In fact, Jesus's hometown people were his toughest critics and did not welcome his message with great enthusiasm.

Family relationships can be touchy and difficult to handle at times. Conflicts can flare up from little things or trivial issues. Work tasks and life responsibilities can create lots of stress and overwhelm everyone in a family. Besides, some families might have to deal with broken relationships or losses of loved ones. What many families need these days is healing. They want God to bring them healing and peace. They ask God to help them accept their family members the way they are without any expectation. They pray that God will help them understand and appreciate one another a little more. They hope that the whole family will learn to care and make sacrifices for one another. What we all need to do is create an atmosphere of love and peace in our family. That way, our family may learn to appreciate one another and heal its past wounds. That is also a wonderful way for us to keep the complaints and criticism in our family down to a minimum.

But love and peace are two attributes that show us God is present in a place, as discussed in the early part of this book. If we come home from a long, hard day at work and see how each family member loves and cares for one another, we certainly see God's presence in this environment. Or when we can recognize the sacrifices and hard work that family members do for one another, we can see God's love and presence in our family. Or when we see that our family knows how to be grateful to God and one another, God is certainly present in the family with such an attitude. One of the best ways for our family to show its gratitude to God and one another is to say grace together before sharing a meal. However, family dinner is not the only opportunity for us to find God. Other family gatherings like baptisms, First Communions, birthdays, graduations, and so on are wonderful occasions for us to meet God also. God surely can be found in other contexts of a home.

Tuesday: Finding God at a School, a Library, or a Center of Education

"St. Francis of Assisi Prayer" by St. Francis of Assisi:

> Lord, make me an instrument of your peace.
> Where there is hatred, let me sow your love;

> where there is injury, pardon; where there is doubt, faith; where there is despair, hope; where there is darkness, light; and where there is sadness, joy. O Divine Master, grant that I may not so much seek to be consoled as to console, to be understood as to understand, to be loved as to love. For it is in giving that we receive, it is in pardoning that we are pardoned, and it is in dying that we are born to eternal life.

We might think that unless we attend a religious academy or school, it will be hard for us to find the divine presence, for we usually assume that God can only be found in a prayerful setting. But the truth is that God can be discovered in an intellectual setting also. We learned that the three wise men studied the constellations and the universe to discover a strange star that led them to baby Jesus, the son of God. Albert Einstein also used his knowledge of physics to discover the mystery of the universe and came to the conclusion that there must be a god who created it and was managing it. Likewise, St. Augustine and St. Thomas relied on their study of philosophy and theology to get to know God better and help others find the way to God. Those are some examples of how God can be found through knowledge over the centuries.

When we use our mind to study and discover God's creation, we will find out and solve lots of life mysteries. Those mysteries will eventually lead us to the heart of God. We will realize that we cannot quite comprehend God with our tiny knowledge. The mystery of God is as deep as the whole universe. However, God has laid its clues all over the universe for us to discover. When we truly use education and knowledge to learn the truth about life and the universe, we will eventually find out more about God, for God is the Creator and sustainer of the universe. It is always exciting to discover new things about the universe or learn something new about life.

That is why school can be a place for us to meet God. Whenever we learn something new, God is present there. Lab technicians or math students might have a divine encountering moment when they solve a problem and find an answer for it. Similarly, people at a library or a bookstore might get so wrapped up in a book because of its fascinating story. They also get delighted to finally solve its mystery and finish a book. Finding out more about God is like solving a mystery or a puzzle. God scatters clues about his identity throughout creation. Every time we discover something new in creation, we discover part of God, and we come a little closer to God. Sometimes, we might have a moment of enlightenment about something. In that moment, we sure have an encounter with God. Knowledge is one of the ways for us to get to know God a little better and hopefully come closer to God.

Wednesday: Finding God at Work, a Repair Shop, a Bank, or a Place of Business

"St. Teresa Prayer" by Teresa of Avila:

> Let nothing disturb thee, nothing affright thee;
> all things are passing; God never changeth;
> Patient endurance attaineth to all things; who
> God possesseth in nothing is wanting; alone
> God sufficeth.

Most of us think that we cannot find God at work unless our workplace is a church, temple, or mosque. But the truth is that God is involved in every aspect of our lives, and we can invite God to show us the way. We can ask God to give us wisdom and a helping hand in dealing with our daily businesses and other challenges. We want the Lord to help us to be truthful and fair in our business dealings. We pray that our life challenges will not overwhelm us and crush our zest for life.

Our work can be a boring and unfulfilling place. We do not see the joy and meaning that it could bring us over the years. Our job nowadays is simply about getting a paycheck. We no longer view our job as the way to touch the lives of others and make a difference in the world. That is how our job can be more than just wage earning, and we can meet God often at work. We should look forward to our workplace every day to see what God might have in store for us. Throughout our busy workday, we might have a moment that gets us to see God in someone or makes us realize God's blessings in our life. Then we definitely have an encounter with God.

Furthermore, if we can see God at work, we can meet God easily when we drop off our car at a repair shop. None of us wants to face a car problem and the cost burden to fix it. The car technician might find more problems with it when we take it there. But we might have a divine encountering moment when we are able to meet a fair and honest car repair shop. Or we might have a pleasant conversation with another person in the shop that can make our day.

Our workday might take us to the bank or some financial institution to have a business transaction. Our account might get scarily low and cause us to worry. But the bank employees might act friendly and treat us well. That might help us realize that God will help us pay all of our bills and take care of our needs. God will give us good health and help us keep our job to have a regular paycheck.

As we deal with our daily businesses, it might take us to a doctor's office or a hospital. Normally, we might not think about God. But if we truly search for God in our daily life, a visit like that might trigger us to pray for a good doctor's report or a complete surgery at the hospital. Those delicate and serious moments help connect us to God and make us realize the importance of God in our life. We will not have to carry our cross alone, for God is ever near us to give us a helping hand and comfort us. By knowing that we have divine assistance in our daily life, we will find the courage and strength to deal with all the issues at hand. It will certainly lift up our spirit and give our souls some peace in challenging situations.

Thursday: Finding God in a Neighborhood or a Place of Charity

"Irish Blessing" (original source unknown):

May the road rise to meet you. May the wind always be at your back. May the sunshine warm upon your face, and the rains fall softly upon your fields, and until we meet again, may God hold you in the palm of his hand.

We might not think God can be found in a neighborhood because of the lack of interactions among its members or because of its diverse beliefs and backgrounds. One neighbor might be Christian or Muslim, while another could be atheist. One neighbor might be loud and untidy, while another could be private and neat. Additionally, everyone can be so busy these days that they do not have time to talk to one another. They also tend to focus only on themselves and their interests at the expense of the common good. They put material things above a good relationship with their neighbors and do not hesitate to create a feud with everyone around. It is hard for us to find the story of the Good Samaritan in our modern-day neighborhood. Neighbors are too busy and private to reach out to help one another. They do not have extra resources to spare for people in need. Moreover, in a highly litigious society like ours, a good deed might cause one neighbor to be sued by another. That discourages some neighbors to lend a helping hand to another in times of need. But having a generous spirit and assisting others with a kind deed is how we can meet God in our daily life. A neighbor that can help mow the grass or blow the snow for another one definitely lets us see the face of God up close and personal, for God often acted generously and helped out the needy in the Bible.

A neighborhood that wants to promote the spirit of unity, peace, and kindness usually comes together to have a party, Christmas lighting, or block sale. In friendly events like those, everyone in the neighborhood comes together to share various activities and get to know one another better. When we see that everyone in a neighborhood cares and helps out one another, we can feel God's presence there. A neighborhood that can come together gives everyone a sense of family and camaraderie. God is definitely present in a united and caring neighborhood.

Some of us might want to take the spirit of that great neighborhood and spread it to a larger community through various charities such as God's Kitchen or Habitat for Humanity. The goal of all charities is to do things and help out others, especially the poor and the misfortunate. If we can take some time out of our busy schedule to help out with a charity, we will have more compassion for our neighbors and meet God more frequently. We will be able to see God in our neighbors and be motivated to serve them joyfully. We will gladly volunteer at God's Kitchen and serve food to the poor there or clean up the place afterward, for those opportunities will remind us of why Jesus washed the feet of his disciples and fed them at the Last Supper. Or when we finish building a home for an underprivileged family with Habitat for Humanity, we can feel like God just completed a wonderful creation for our human family. Most of us can meet God easily when we volunteer our service for a charity. Our great feeling afterward confirms to us that we have had a divine encounter or experience.

Friday: Finding God at a Ball Game, a Theater, or a Center of Entertainment

"The Beauty of Creation Bears Witness to God" Prayer by St. Augustine:

Question the beauty of the earth, the beauty of the sea, the beauty of the wide air around you, the beauty of the sky; question the order of the stars, the sun whose brightness lights the day, the moon whose splendor softens the gloom of night; question the living creatures that move in the waters, that roam upon the earth, that fly through the air; the spirit that lies hidden, the matter that is manifest; the visible things that are ruled, the visible that rule them; question all these. They will answer you: "Behold and see, we are beautiful." Their beauty is their confession of God. Who made these beautiful changing things, if not one who is beautiful and changeth not?

Many people think that God can only be found in a caring neighborhood or a peaceful place like a church or temple. But the truth is that God can be seen everywhere, including at a ball game, a theater, or a center of entertainment. Places like those are often loud, noisy, crowded, and full of sense stimulants. Those elements can drown out any sign of God's presence. That is the greatest challenge for us in modern-day society as we try to search for God amidst all the noises and distractions of our high-tech world.

We can find God at a ball game when we see the biblical sign John 3:16 on the field or when our children huddle together for a quick prayer and ask God to bless the game and keep everyone safe. But God can be seen in things other than the huddled prayer. When we see a referee or an umpire calling the game fairly and challenging all the players to exercise good sportsmanship, they help us see the real face of God at a public event. God's presence can also be found at a ball game when we see kind acts or meet an old friend.

We often think a theater or an appropriate center of entertainment is just a place for relaxation and enjoyment. But we can find God's presence in a venue like that when we meet kind and courteous people, for they remind us of how God would treat us and call us to do the same. They let us have a glimpse of God and announce to us about God's constant presence in our world. That glimpse makes us forget about our life burdens for a moment and calls us to enjoy some downtime with our family and friends.

But kindness and friendship are not the only two ways for us to meet God at a ball game, a theater, or a center of entertainment. When we relax at one of those venues and refresh our spirit after a long, hard work week, we will have a good chance to meet God, for God took time to rest after the tough work of creating the universe, as the Bible tells us. Even Jesus reminded his disciples to get some rest and renew their spirit after a long, hard day at work, for God cannot communicate to us when we are exhausted, anxious, or worried. God wants us to be peaceful, joyful, and refreshed. Indeed, St. Augustine's spirit was restless as he searched for God in various forms of pleasure. Only after he found God was his spirit at peace. He tells us about the connection between a renewed spirit and God's presence as follows: "My soul is restless until it rests in you[,] my God."

Saturday: Finding God at a Shopping Mall, a Grocery Store, or a Public Place

"I See His Blood Upon the Rose" by Joseph M. Plunkett:

I see his blood upon the rose and in the stars the glory of his eyes; his body gleams amid eternal snows, his tears fall from the skies. I see his face in every flower; the thunder and the singing of the birds are but his voice—and carven by his power rocks are his written words. All pathways by his feet are worn, his strong heart stirs the ever-beating sea, his crown of thorns is twined with every thorn, and his cross is every tree.

Shopping is a way of life for all Americans. Our week would not be complete without making a trip to a store to shop for something. We shop for food, drink, gas, basic necessities, clothes, and other personal items. We look forward to the holidays to give us more reasons to shop for ourselves and our loved ones. But our busy lifestyle and crammed daily schedule might make our trips to the stores rushed, tense, and almost impossible. We cannot find what we want from the store in a timely manner. We get frustrated to see that the prices for some items are outrageously high. We become impatient waiting in a long checkout line. We feel uneasy when customer service personnel does not treat us courteously. If we run into one of those problems with shopping, we have tough time finding God in a store. What we find is just hassle, frustration, fighting, and trampling on other shoppers, especially during the holidays.

However, we can find God and other wonderful virtues on our shopping trips. When people do not fight or act rudely in a store, we might have witnessed God's presence there. Or we might get lucky and find all the items we need at a discount price. That certainly brings joy to our hearts, and God is definitely present in moments like that. Or we might meet an old friend or neighbor at the store and the odds for something like that to happen are very rare. That miracle tells us that God is present in our midst, and God made that impossible meeting happen. Or we might be able to help an elderly person or someone in the store get something. Our kind and humble act shows others God's love, and without a doubt, God is present in the store. Or we might see a parent show love and mercy to his or her misbehaving child while attempting to discipline him or her. That is what God does to us every day. Surely we can see God's presence in that gentle and caring parent.

There are other opportunities or situations in the store that might help us have an encounter with God. If we know how to search for God in any type of situation around us, we will surely meet God a lot in our daily life, even at a busy shopping store.

Sunday: Finding God at a Church, a Temple, or a Mosque

"Lead, Kindly Light" by Cardinal John Henry Newman:

Lead, kindly Light, amid the encircling gloom, lead thou me on; the night is dark, and I am far from home, lead thou me on. Keep thou my feet; I do not ask to see the distant scene; one step enough for me. I was not ever thus, nor prayed that thou shouldst lead me on; I loved to choose and see my path; but now lead thou me on. I loved the garish day, and, spite of fears, pride ruled my will: remember not past years. So long thy power hath blest me, sure it still will lead me on o'er moor and fen, o'er crag and torrent, till the night is gone, and with the morn those angel faces smile, which I have loved long since, and lost awhile.

If there is one place we certainly find God, it is the church, temple, or mosque. It is surely easier for us to find God in a sacred place like that than other settings. Being in God's presence makes us forget about our life troubles for a moment and takes us to a different world. We feel elated and at peace when we are in God's presence. That is why many of us love to stop by a church, temple, or mosque throughout the week to experience a moment of peace. After a long, hard day at work, what we need the most is some peace. We come to church, temple, or mosque to unload our heavy hearts to God and clear up our confused minds. We might have worries, anxieties, or concerns about something. We might be upset or sad over some daily issues. We might feel lost or confused on what we should do at certain moments of our lives. So we come to church, temple, or mosque to find peace and solutions for our problems. For we know that the only one who can bring us true peace for our souls and solutions for our lives is God. We feel relieved and peaceful after spending some time with God in a sacred place. Indeed, we have met God, and the result of it is a renewed spirit.

However, peace and solutions are not the only reasons to draw us to church, temple, or mosque. We also come to those places because we want to belong to a community and feel connected with others. A church, temple, or mosque helps unite everyone from various backgrounds and cultures and gathers them into a family. God is indeed the source of unity. When we feel connected to a community, we have had an encounter with God. A church, temple, or mosque community may also give its members a sense of security and joy. As we feel safe, secure, and joyful in a community of faith, we certainly have found God in that way, for God always makes us feel safe and brings joy to our lives.

CHAPTER 5

HOW AN ORDINARY PERSON FINDS GOD IN EXTRAORDINARY SITUATIONS

It is often difficult for us to find God in our daily life, for God is quite subtle in revealing his presence. Besides, we often get distracted by many things around us every day. Our family and work might demand our full attention at times and take most of our time. We do not have time and energy each day to find God, even though we know that we need God in our lives. God is the strength and guide for us as we continue our earthly journey.

If we struggle to see God around us every day, it might be much more difficult for us to find God in extraordinary situations, for those situations will turn our lives upside down and create more hurdles to keep us from meeting God. In the following section, we will try to figure out how to find God in extraordinary situations.

Tragedies

These situations usually cause us pain and hurt. They pop out of nowhere and catch us by surprise. Some of them might be personal, while others are national. Some personal tragedies can be caused by cars, airplanes, fires, gun, work equipment, drug overdoses, and so on. They happen to our families, friends, neighbors, coworkers, or people we know. Meanwhile, national tragedies can be 9/11, school bombings, random shootings at some public venue, national disasters, and so on. These events often bring us sadness, hurt, and losses. In moments like that, we find it difficult to see God's presence in our midst.

But what Mary and early disciples teach us is that an Easter miracle and a new life can happen after a huge tragedy, like it did for the death and burial of their Lord Jesus. They thought the tragic death of their master was so painful that they could not move on with their lives and assigned mission. While they were still mourning over the sad loss of their friend Jesus, the Holy Spirit appeared to give them courage and strength to move out of the upper room and go on with Christ's mission of salvation. With time and divine grace, they were able to reconnect their relationship with God and find a new life. God's grace helped them heal up and leave their tragic past behind so that they could write up a new chapter of their lives by their mission work around the world. They all were able to meet the risen Christ later on, including a doubting Thomas.

Similarly, we will be able to leave our tragic past behind and heal up with the help of time and divine grace. Our wound from a tragedy needs time to heal. Only with God's grace will we find peace for our wounded soul and a new life for our future. We will learn to reconnect with God and ask the Holy Spirit to give us courage and strength to continue on with our lives. We will be able to leave our tragic past behind and try to write up a new chapter of our lives. In that process of searching for healing and a new life, we will find God. Like a doubting Thomas, we will have to confess, "My Lord and my God," when we meet the risen Christ or have the Easter moment. We will experience peace and joy upon our divine encounter, as Mary Magdalene and all the disciples did.

Sickness

Most of us do not like to see our doctors or go to the hospital, for we do not want to find out our health problems or be confined in a depressing place like a hospital. If a tragedy is a devastating blow to us, a diagnosis of an illness might be a death sentence. We all want to be healthy and remain strong on our life journey. None of us likes to be sick. It would be a painful reality if we had to suffer with some sort of illness. Our normal life and daily routines would be turned upside down. We would not be able to do simple things that a normal person could. We would have to call out for help for everything. We would ask our doctors for the right treatments and look for the best solutions to get rid of our illness and be normal like healthy people. We hate to be isolated and feel alone due to our sickness. We need to call on God to heal us and restore our health.

In the Gospels, we see that the sick and afflicted came to Jesus either as the first choice or as the last resort. They brought him all sorts of health problems. Some were deaf and mute, while others were paralyzed. Some suffered from leprosy, while others were possessed by evil spirits. Several people even came to him to ask for healing on behalf of someone else. They all had faith in Jesus and his ability to heal them. The moment they meet Jesus, they found God, for they believed he had divine origin and was either the long-awaited Messiah or the most respected prophet of all time. If anyone who could perform a miracle and heal them, it would be Jesus. When they experienced his healing power and witnessed his miracles, they knew immediately God was with them. They were overjoyed and could not stop sharing the wonderful news with the public. The people poured out in great numbers toward Jesus in many towns and villages, and he could not enter some places in secret.

Similarly, many of us have experienced healing every day, from a cold to a minor cut. But we often wait till a major health event and a huge healing success for us to recognize God's presence in our lives. When we come out of a major surgery successfully or hear the news from our doctors that we are free of cancer, we certainly have met God at that moment. Unfortunately, sometimes our illness is terminal after we have exhausted all treatments. It is hard for us to accept that end result. Yet as long as we can accept it and make peace with ourselves through the help of God's grace and the support of our loved ones, we definitely have met God. That experience gives us a sense of peace and relief. That is a sign of God's presence among us.

Broken relationships

If there is one thing that might be tough for us to face after our sickness and tragedies, it is a broken relationship. That could be a divorce, separation, death, strange family dynamic, and so on. If we have ever gotten caught in a tangled mess of relationships, we know how painful and depressing this situation can be on us. It takes lots of resources from us and drains our energy. It brings bad memories and can touch raw nerves. We would be glad to fix up our broken relationships and put an end to them. That would be the best solution for this apparent problem. There are many examples in the Bible to guide and console us through this life situation. The best Bible example is the story of the prodigal son. We could see how painful it was for the caring father to see his youngest son wander away from his family. This estranged relationship caused lots of worry and anxiety in the concerned father. It also brought tension and resentment with the oldest son. He had to carry on all the heavy work and responsibilities for the family. The loving father would have loved to see his prodigal son come home and be reconciled with the whole family. His prayer thankfully was answered, and the prodigal son came home to reconcile with his family. The moment that the lost son embraced his father was the time he met God. The day he reconciled with his father was the time he found God again in his life. But as we might recall, reconciliation with the whole family would take time because the oldest son refused to enter the house and shake hands with his brother. He also kept telling his father his grievances and referring to his brother as "your son."

Similarly, when we are able to reconcile with someone, we definitely meet God at that moment. Anytime we can mend a broken relationship, we certainly find God then. Many Biblical stories use the image of the lost sheep and the good shepherd to show us the importance of reconciliation and presence of God in those moments. We can only imagine how relieved we would feel when we made peace with someone. The peace and joy we find in relationships and people around us shows God's presence. It is our goal to turn all of our relationships into a source of peace and joy. When we are able to do that, especially with the broken relationships, we will have a better chance of meeting God more regularly. We will also be able to experience lots of wonderful miracles by our encounters with God.

Daily Problems

Our lives would be quite boring if we did not have to deal with daily problems. They range from family problems to work issues. Family problems can be something wrong with the house, car problems, sick kids, or misbehaving kids. Work issues can be unfriendly bosses, a stressful working environment, unbearable coworkers, and so on. Those daily issues can create frustration and bring stress into our daily life. When we get frustrated, we might say hurtful things and do things we might regret later. Life burdens and daily stress can also make our day long and miserable. But if we can find God throughout our day, God might be able to help us stay calm, cool, and collected under the overwhelming pressure and responsibilities of our day. We might even feel joyful and energetic on a hectic day. We could also see all the little miracles throughout the day and could not wait to welcome new ones.

We can meet God on a hectic day by taking a quick moment to pray and give thanks to God for something. Sometimes, we might meet God by encountering an honest, kind, and generous person in the course of the day. Just like God, this type of person is special and rare for us to find in our dog-eat-dog world. Sometimes, we might meet God when a few things go well for us on our tough day. Our house or car problem might get fixed quickly, and we are given a discount rate. Or the traffic lights might wait for us to go through before turning red. Or our bosses and coworkers might unexpectedly be nice to us on this rough day. Every nice thing that happens to us on a hectic day is a sign of God's presence in our world. We must be able to recognize it and acknowledge it with a short prayer. That is how we can stay connected to God continuously and receive God's abundant blessings and miracles.

Other Unusual Situations

Besides tragedies, broken relationships, and daily problems, we might have to face loneliness, depression, worry, or anxiety. All those issues can easily keep us away from recognizing God's presence in our daily life and make us feel lost in this world. We sure need help from above to face this personal cross and return to normal again. The best way for us to meet God is to find a supportive community in our family, friends, and people of faith. That community will encourage us and help us figure out how to find hope and joy in our daily life. It will also reach out to lend us a helping hand and show us the way forward. It is the life raft God sends us to guide us safely to the land of joy and peace. That supportive community is a sign of God's presence with us when we feel lonely, depressed, worried, or anxious. With the support of a community, we can rely on others to help us in challenging times. We feel more confident and relieved in dealing with our daily hassles. We will be motivated to go on with our day and complete our daily duties.

However, sometimes God's presence is a little more subtle and takes on the form of caring friends or kind neighbors. They are like angels God has sent our way to bring us comfort and help us move forward. Sometimes, we take their kind acts for granted. Or we might assume regular people would always reach out and do nice things for others. But the fact is that most people do not. We need to recognize those kind deeds and thank God for directing people like that to us. We must not overlook those kind angels and must embrace them wholeheartedly, for they might come by our home to spend time with us and help us with whatever we might need. They also make us laugh and cheer us on in our dreams and hopes. Or they could guide us through tough days and make us believe in ourselves again. Those friends and neighbors surely represent God's presence and come to our aid in difficult times. They also help us celebrate life and enjoy it much more.

But God's presence can be found beyond our friends, neighbors, and community when we have to face some unusual situations. Sometimes, his presence might come in the form of a good day—namely, everything goes our way. Other times, it might appear from unlikely sources around us, such as generous strangers and kind neighbors. We just need to search diligently and pay more attention to places other than churches, temples, and mosques. There, we will meet God and find the needed divine help. Like hidden treasure, it will be a wonderful blessing and great joy for us if we can find God in our daily life in spite of the circumstances we might face.

The potential rewards for us would be huge when they happen. We will have the protection and safeguards we need against any danger and harm. We will get the necessary source of guidance and counsel to make the right decisions and do the right things in challenging times. We will always have peace and joy in our hearts no matter how our life situations might turn out. We will have the strength and courage to get up each day and continue the mission God has assigned us, for we are not alone. God is by our side to guide us and walk with us. God will show us lots of wonderful miracles on our faith journey. God is indeed the hidden precious treasure that we humans have dreamt about and searched for since the beginning of creation. May we keep on searching for God every moment of our life and be rewarded handsomely for it. May we find the precious treasure hidden in God that will bring us true peace and happiness right here in this life.

BOOKS FOR SALE

$13.95 (Inspirational Read)

$11.95 (Spiritual Read)

$17.95 (Adult Daily Devotion)

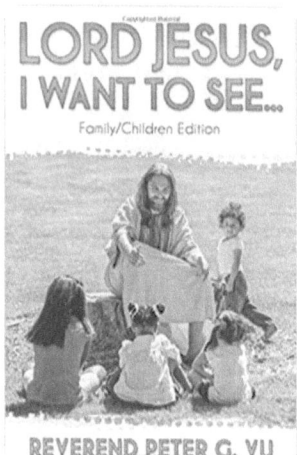

$12.95 (Family/Children Devotion)

$6.99 (Children/Adventure Read) $5.99 (Children/Adventure Read)

(Inspiration/Wisdom Read)   (Children/Adventure Read)

You can find books at:
www.theewingspublishing.com; www.HaynesMediaGroup.com;
www.aegadesign.com; www.BarnesandNoble.com;
www.Amazon.com.

www.ingramcontent.com/pod-product-compliance
Lightning Source LLC
Chambersburg PA
CBHW021448070526
44577CB00002B/308